1st Steps for a Beginning Guitarist

Volume One
Chords and Chord Progressions

By
Bruce Arnold

Muse Eek Publishing Company
New York, New York

ISBN 1-890944-90-4

Library of Congress Card Number: 2001116023

Printed in the United States

This publication can be purchased from your local bookstore or by contacting:
Muse Eek Publishing Company
P.O. Box 509
New York, NY 10276, USA
Phone: 212-473-7030
Fax: 212-473-4601
http://www.muse-eek.com
sales@muse-eek.com

Table Of Contents

Quick Start

There are many ways to approach this book. The important thing is that sooner or later you should read and understand everything presented. Each individual works differently and is at a different level, so here are some possible ways of approaching this book.

TOTAL BEGINNER: I have no previous experience playing the guitar or with music in general.

1. Read pages 1-4 while referring to the pictures on pages 51-2 and video files on muse.eek.com
2. Tune your guitar using method on pages 5-6 or use internet guitar tuning files on muse-eek.com
3. Read pages 18-19 and start learning the chords on pages 19-26.
4. When you take a break start reading the music theory section on page 9-17 and the understanding rhythm on pages 32-5
5. As you feel more comfortable with the chords and understand rhythm start learning the chord progressions on pages 37-48.

INTERMEDIATE BEGINNER: I have played a while but know very little.

1. Read pages 1-4 while referring to the pictures on pages 51-2 understand that one of reasons you might have had problems in the past playing the guitar is because your technique is flawed. Look for your problems by comparing notes with the book and looking in a mirror to see how you are playing. Also check video files on muse.eek.com
2. Check page 18 for explanation of chord diagrams and then proceed to explanation of chord progression on page 36.
3. Begin working on chord progression on pages 37-48 refer to pages 32-35 if you have rhythm problems.

ADVANCED BEGINNER: I know most "open" position chords but can't play songs yet.

1. Read pages 1-4 while referring to the pictures on pages 51-2 and video files on muse.eek.com and start to correct any discrepancies you find in your technique.
2. Read page 36 and start learning the chord progressions.
3. When you take a break start reading the music theory section on page 9-17 and the Understanding Rhythm on pages 32-5.
4. Read pages 27-28 and learn all barre chords on pages 29-31 using the cycle 5 progression.

Master these things over time

1. Read and reread the music theory section on pages 9-17 until in makes sense to you.
2. Learn all "open" chords and use the cycle 5 progression on 28 to memorize all "barre" chords
3. Read and reread the Understand Rhythm section of page 32-5 until you can play the examples.
4. Keep rereading pages 1-4 and check your technique in a mirror or with a video camera.
5. Start to memorize the notes of the guitar fretboard on page 8.

Hint: When I was first trying to memorize the notes on the guitar fretboard, I photocopied a page like page 8 and carried it around with me. I would quiz myself while walking, or sitting on a train. For example: What note is on the 6th fret of the D string? I would then check my answers with the diagram of the fretboard to make sure I was correct.

About the Author

Bruce Arnold is from Sioux Falls, South Dakota. His educational background started with 3 years of music study at the University of South Dakota; he then attended the Berklee College of Music where he received a Bachelor of Music degree in composition. During that time he also studied privately with Jerry Bergonzi and Charlie Banacos.

Mr. Arnold has taught at some of the most prestigious music schools in America, including the New England Conservatory of Music, Dartmouth College, Berklee College of Music, Princeton University and New York University. He has also had extensive experience teaching beginning students of the guitar. He has taught in the Community Extension Programs that target beginning students of all ages at The New England Conservatory of music. His experience teaching high school students at the prestigious St. Paul's Preparatory school along with numerous clinics nationwide has given him added insights into the beginning student's needs.

Along with his teaching credentials Mr. Arnold has an impressive performance background, and he gigs regularly in the New York area. Currently he is performing with his own "The Bruce Arnold Trio," and "Eye Contact" with Harvie Swartz, as well as with two experimental bands, "Release the Hounds" a free improv group, and "Spooky Actions" which re-interprets the work of 20th Century classical masters. His debut CD "Blue Eleven" (MMC 2036J) received great critical acclaim, and his most recent CD "A Few Dozen" was released in January 2000. The Los Angeles Times said of this release "Mr. Arnold deserves credit for his effort to expand the jazz palette."

For more information about Mr. Arnold check his website at arnoldjazz.com This website contains audio examples of Mr. Arnold's compositions and a workshop section with free downloadable music exercises.

Foreword

    This book has been created for the beginning guitarist who wants to start out with the proper techniques and directions in order to reach his or her full potential in music. The importance of learning the right physical and mental approaches to music and how they relate to the guitar cannot be overly stressed. If you start with the right information you will see steady, unhampered improvement. Almost all the problems I see in guitarists (including myself) have come from basic misconceptions and bad suggestions from previous teachers or books. It's not enough for a book or teacher to say "use the pick to strike the strings." You need to show the student exactly how the pick should be held, and how the muscles of the hand are involved to lay the foundations of proper technique. This book gets into these specifics; master them and you will surely reach a high level of proficiency. In some cases you might need to spend a little more time getting a particular technique down before proceeding, but this will pay off and make all the difference. <u>Haste makes waste</u>, and the line of guitarists wondering why they can't play well or why they can't play fast, why they haven't improved in years, or why they have pain when they play is long. It is also recommended that you read the "Further Thoughts on Practicing and Playing Music" on page 50 before starting this book.

    Muse Eek Publishing has created a website with a FAQ forum for all my books. If you have any questions about anything contained in this book feel free to contact me at FAQ@muse-eek.com and I will happy to post an answer to your question. My goal is to educate you, and help you to reach a higher degree of musical ability.

Bruce Arnold
New York, New York

Important Background Information

If you have just purchased a guitar or received one as a present it is important to first understand some basic general information that will help you get off on the right foot. The concepts presented here are really the most important thing you will ever learn on the guitar. It is sad but true, that with most of the new students I receive, I usually spend the first year correcting problems. Nine out of ten times these problems were caused by not knowing the proper technique to use on the guitar or not understanding the right way to process music both intellectually and aurally. This book will help you get started in the right way so you can develop to your full potential.

A picture is worth a thousand words, so for many of the concepts presented here you will find pictures on pages 51-2 and short videos on the muse-eek.com website found under the book's title listing. Some exercises can also be found as midifiles or mp3 files, just like a teacher would demonstrate in a lesson, so you can hear what the exercise should sound like and see the techniques discussed with your own eyes. I urge you to download these pictures and videos to your computer so you can examine them closely and refer back to each file for further refinement of each technique presented. As an owner of this book you also have free access to this "member's section." Take advantage of this, because you will find other information and educational files to help you develop as a musician.

The first step in playing the guitar is to learn such basic information as how to tune a guitar, hold your pick properly and position your hands and body in relationship to the guitar to help you play correctly so as not to develop any repetitive stress injuries. We will also discuss some of the basic concepts of strumming the guitar and where notes are located on the guitar neck. A music theory section is also included to get you started thinking about music in a structured way. This theory section will be quite challenging for the beginning student. Don't feel like you have to master the music theory before moving on to the chords and chord progressions. If you have problems with the music theory, just relax and keep rereading it until it makes sense to you. The important thing is that in this book you have all the information to get you started in the right direction.

This book can't cover every subject at the depth you will need. Along the way I will recommend other books for study which will help you correct problems or enrich your understanding. Don't automatically figure you are untalented if you run into a road block. If you have a particular problem try using some of the books or e-books I recommend for further study. You could also check the FAQ section for this book and see if others have had similar problems, or contact me and I will make suggestions to help you get on the right track again.

Care of your Guitar

Let's discuss the care of your guitar. It's your "baby" so take care of it.

Store your guitar in the case. If you leave it sitting out anywhere, you are inviting problems, from having some bozo grabbing your guitar and messing it up, to things getting dropped on it, to falling over it and breaking it. Why take the chance?

In the winter time don't store your guitar near an active heater. Dry air will crack the wood of your instrument. Try to keep you house or apartment between 30 and 40 percent humidity. If this is impossible buy a humidifier for your guitar. You can find these in any music store. They are very cheap but they do the trick.

If you lean your guitar against a wall (which I don't recommend) put the string side facing the wall, not the back. This usually gives the guitar more stability and makes it less likely to fall over.

Try to avoid extreme changes in temperature when transporting your guitar. If you take your guitar to a friend's house in the winter time, let the guitar warm up for 15 to 20 minutes before taking it out of the case.

All these tips will go a long way towards keeping your guitar safe and in one piece for many years.

Holding the Guitar

There are two methods of holding the guitar. You basic position will either be sitting or standing. If you are sitting you want to place the guitar across your lap and rest the inward curving section of the guitar on your right or left leg. (See picture 7 or video clip 3 for different views of this position) The "classical" technique for holding the guitar is to place it on the left leg, spreading your legs and allowing the rest of the body of the guitar to fall between your two legs. I would highly recommend using this technique if you are sitting down. This will help you maintain the proper position for both your right and left hands. You should also raise up your left leg about 3 to 5 inches. This can be done by placing your foot on the guitar case. The height of this foot rest will vary from person to person. As a basic guideline you don't want to put the foot rest so high that you are forced to raise your left shoulder to reach up to the neck. Anything that will support your leg is fine. There are adjustable guitar footrests that you can purchase in any music store which are obviously the best to have, because you can get the exact height that is comfortable for you. If you put a strap on later and stand up, your guitar should be in the same position on your body as it was when your were sitting. Practice the way you will perform. I get many guitarists who can't figure out why they play so much better when they are sitting at home in a chair, than they do when performing or rehearsing standing up. It's because they are holding their guitar in one position when they are practicing, and a different position when performing. It's just common sense to practice the way you will perform but you'd be amazed how many people don't realize this. If you are playing an electric guitar you can use the same technique but quite honestly, you would be much better off standing and using a strap. It's very seldom that an electric guitarist performs sitting down, so don't practice while sitting down. You should adjust your strap so that the middle of the back of the guitar falls around your belly button. Each person is built differently so exact placement will have to be found but a good indicator is actually what your left hand position ends up being on the guitar. (See photo 10)

The Left Hand/Arm Position

Your left hand should come around the neck from below it. Your shoulder should be relaxed. (See photo 1,5,7 and 10 or video clip 3) It is very common for students to raise, clench or hold their shoulder up. If your strap is too high you will find you are raising your shoulder. You will also find your shoulder is to high if you are sitting and you have your left foot raised too high. Your fingers should be relaxed. I often tell students to first put your hand down by your side and let it relax. Then bring the hand up to the guitar neck. Your hand should remain in the same relaxed position. Fingers should be relaxed, and the wrist should be straight. (See photo 1 -6 and video clip 3) If you find that your wrist is getting bent at more than a 10 to 20 degree angle when you are playing notes on the guitar, you need to raise the height of the guitar up so your wrist will not be forced into that angle. People who play over long periods of time with their wrist bent at too much of an angle will find that they develop pain, and sooner or later a repetitive stress injury. (See photos 1-4, 5, 6 and video clip 3 for proper wrist angle)

A common mistake students make is to stretch their fingers out so that one finger is covering each fret. **Don't** do this. I give students this example when considering how to place your left hand on the guitar. Hold your left hand out in front of you and stretch your fingers apart. Now try and move your fingers and feel how flexible they are. Next, relax you hand by the side of your body and then bring it out in front of your body. Now try moving your fingers. You will find that a relaxed hand allows your fingers to move more quickly and with less tension. This is how your hand should be when you are playing the guitar. Relaxed, with fingers relatively close to each other. (See video clip 7)

There are of course examples of particular melodies and chords that will require you to stretch your fingers out. (I sometimes get students who bring me a particular musical example where they don't understand how it could be played without stretching the fingers out.) But your basic

2

position should always be one of relaxed fingers fairly close together. I have never seen a great guitarist who played with a tense hand. One last point to keep in mind is that each person is different. If you have very short fingers a stretch for you might not be a stretch for someone with very long fingers.

The next common question is: How do I move from one note to another if I don't stretch my hand out? This is accomplished by a combination of elbow and shoulder action that moves your hand up and down the neck to reach each fret. This technique will take some time to develop but it keeps your fingers in the same relationship to the neck as you play each note. At this point it can't be over emphasized how important it is to keep your hand and fingers in a consistent relationship to the guitar fretboard. Many students play the guitar differently depending where they are on the guitar neck . This makes playing the guitar a lot harder. By maintaining the same position you are honing in on one technique, and by maintaining a consistent, relaxed technique you will develop speed and precision on the guitar. (See video clip 2-7)

The Left Hand Finger Position

You will be playing using the tips of your fingers and your fingers should be slightly arched. (See photos 1-2,12 and video clip 2-7) This is the usual position of your hand when it is relaxed by the side of your body. When you press down on a note you want to press between the frets to make a note sound. You only want to press hard enough to make the note sound. Most students press too hard with their left hand when playing notes. Spend some time analyzing the way your hand is working and make sure you are not pressing too hard. The harder you press, the slower you will play, and the faster your hand will tire.

The Right Hand/Arm Position

Your right hand should come over the body of the guitar. (See photos 7 and 10.) Keep your shoulders relaxed and guard against the tendency to raise them up. Your arm from the elbow to the tips of your fingers should be straight using your elbow to raise or lower your arm to play each string. (See photos 7 and 10 and video clip 2.) The forearm (the area between the wrist and elbow) should be used to pick each string. This forearm movement is the same movement used to drink a glass of water, turn a screw driver or open a door. Another way to experience this movement is to lay your arm flat on a table and lift your thumb up using your forearm. Don't use the muscle in your thumb but allow your forearm to pick your thumb up off the table. This technique will seem a little awkward to begin with but by using the big muscle group in your forearm you will have the power and endurance to play for long periods of time without injury. (See video clip 8)

It should be mentioned that many students use their wrists to pick each note. I have found that though this technique will work, you do run the risk of injury. The wrist contains very small muscles and they are easily damaged. Also a tendency to hold your arm stationary and just move your wrist up and down to play each string is inviting disaster. This is the same motion that creates Carpal Tunnel Syndrome when using a mouse on a computer.

Many guitarists try to rest one or more of their fingers against the body of the guitar to help them get a "feel" for where the strings are. I have seen nothing but problems develop later on using this technique. I strongly recommend that you not rely on your hand touching the guitar. Keep your fingers relaxed. Your arm from the upper forearm to the elbow should be the only place where your arm touches the guitar. This will allow your lower forearm, wrist and hand to move freely. (See photo 7)

Using a Guitar Pick

The type of pick you use is a personal preference. Go to a local music store and buy one light , one medium and one heavy gauge pick. They are very cheap, so by a bunch if you're up for it. Try each pick for a week or two and see which one feels the best and which one sounds the best. I use an extra heavy pick because I like the resistance, sound and feel. But that is just me. You are the final judge as to what feels and sounds best for you; There is no right or wrong pick weight.

You should hold the pick either between your thumb and first finger or the thumb and your first and second finger together. (See photos 8-9) Students commonly press their fingers together too tightly while gripping the pick. This can cause tension in the forearm. Keep the rest of your fingers relaxed. If you start to feel pain or stress in your fingers or forearm you are probably holding the pick too tightly.

When you pick the string you do not want to dig your pick too far into the strings, because this will slow you down. Compare photos 15 and 16. In photo 16 the pick is picking too far into the string. Photo 15 is the correct method.

To recap: your right arm/elbow combination will be doing the work of strumming. Strumming refers to the technique you use to play all the notes in chords. You usually start from the lower in pitch strings and move the pick across the strings in a downward motion. You can also strum with an upward motion. You will need both as you start to play the chords to different songs. You can initiate the strum from your elbow or your forearm. I use mostly my forearm and a little movement of the elbow. When picking individual strings you will use your forearm and then your elbow to move up or down to the next string. (See video clip 1, 2 and 8.)

Applying Right and Left Hand Techniques

For a technical application of right and left hand technique I would recommend the following: First, overall try to apply your new technique to everything you have learned so far on the guitar. For some this is a daunting task if you have been playing for a while. But you will find that whether you are a beginner or a seasoned pro after awhile this technique will feel natural and music that you already know will quickly fall into place. More specifically for both left and right hand technique I recommend downloading the major scales, arpeggios and sweeps from the "Music Workshop" at www.arnoldjazz.com, following the directions on each page. Also for right hand technique I have written a book called "Right Hand Technique for Guitar Volume One" ISBN 096486326X. This book will give you hundreds of right hand exercises.

Pictures and Videos

Along with the pictures found on pages 51-52 you will find video clips under this book's title on the muse-eek.com website. Take full advantage of these visual aids as they will help you understand the proper technique on the guitar. An extra few weeks spent refining your basic interface with the guitar will help you to progress more productively. You will also find that any music you play sounds better when your muscles are relaxed and being used in the right way. You will also avoid the injuries that can arise from incorrect technique.

Other Guitar Information

Change your guitar strings at least once every six months. New strings bring life back into an instrument. There are many different gauges and types of strings. The lighter the strings the easier they are to play but you sacrifice tone and volume as you use lighter and lighter strings . Bring your guitar with you when you buy your first set and have the clerk help you with string selection. Guitar strings come in pregauged sets. These sets of 6 strings are listed as different gauges. In general I would recommend medium to light string sets for both an acoustic and electric guitar.

Keep in mind that an acoustic guitar is traditionally harder to play than an electric guitar because of the higher string tension found on most acoustics. Therefore if you are working through this book with an acoustic guitar give yourself some extra time for your hand to get use to the extra pressure needed to push down the strings.

Tuning the Guitar

First, let's look at the basic mechanics of the guitar before starting to tune. There are tuning pegs at the far end of the guitar neck. Turning these pegs will raise or lower the pitch of the string. Play each string with your right hand and locate the peg that changes the pitch of that corresponding string. Over time you will know which peg changes which string but it isn't unusual to be confused about these pegs when you are first starting out.

If you take your right hand and play each string without using your left hand, you are playing on what is referred to as the "open" strings. To play other notes you need to press your left hand down on a string. When you do this you need to place one of your fingers between one of the frets and play that corresponding string with your right hand. When you play a note in this manner you are said to be "fretting" a note. In order to tune the guitar you are going to use a combination of playing an open string and comparing it to a "fretted" pitch on an neighboring string. The Figure 1 shows you a guitar neck with some of the basic information you will need to know to get started.

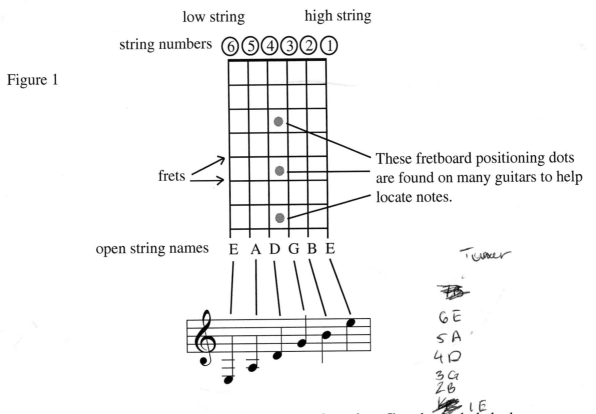

Figure 1

These fretboard positioning dots are found on many guitars to help locate notes.

Notice each string has a corresponding name and number. I've also included where you would find these open string pitches on a musical staff. We will discuss the music staff later.

There are many ways to tune a guitar. You can use an electronic guitar tuning device, or a pitch pipe either of which can be purchased at a music store. Although I use an electronic guitar tuner when I perform I recommend you start to develop the ability to tune your guitar by hearing the sounds. For a beginner this can be a frustrating procedure. It takes time to develop your ear to recognize whether or not your guitar is in tune. The basic concept of tuning a stringed instrument is to make two pitches sound the same. In the case of the guitar we fret one string and play another to try to make the two notes, i.e. strings, sound the same. As you work on this you will find your ability to hear whether two notes sound exactly the same will improve. Don't worry if at first you feel like you are a lost cause. Many beginning students have problems first discerning whether two pitches are the same and also have problems with the basic mechanics of the tuning process.

5

As a first step you will need to tune one of your strings to the correct pitch (often referred to as a "concert pitch." Do this by either using another instrument like a piano, tuning fork or guitar tuner. If none of these are immediately available you can tune your guitar anyway (as long as it is close to concert pitch) and it just won't be in the correct "concert pitch." This means that if you try to play with another guitarist you won't be tuned the same, and it will not sound good. If you are playing by yourself you may not notice any problem at all. **There is, however, a tuning pitch for each open string on the muse-eek.com website that you can play with the free downloadable midifile player. Most browsers like Netscape and Explorer will also play midifiles. In addition there are mp3 files of a guitar playing each open string to help you get your guitar in tune. You will find these files under the book's title listing.**

Using one of the previously mentioned methods, tune your 6th or low E string. As I mentioned we are going to play one "open" string and compare that pitch's sound to a fretted note on an adjacent string. To tune the A (5th string) we are going to play an A note on the low E string (6th string) by placing our index finger on the 5th fret of the low E string and then play the open A string (5th string). (See Diagram 1). Play both strings. See if the A string sounds lower or higher in pitch. If the A string sounds lower in pitch raise the string up using the tuning peg for the A string until both strings sound the same. Conversely if the A string's pitch sounds too high in pitch, lower it using the tuning peg until both strings sound the same.

Diagram 1

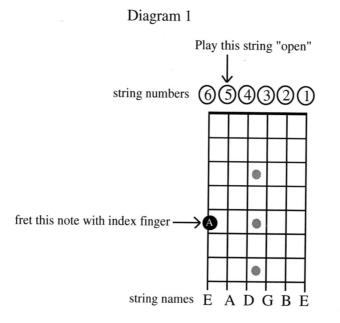

We will now continue this process for each string, always comparing the fretted string to the next higher "open" string. Notice that when you tune the G string to the B string you press on the 4th fret note the 5th. (See Diagram 4 on the next page.)

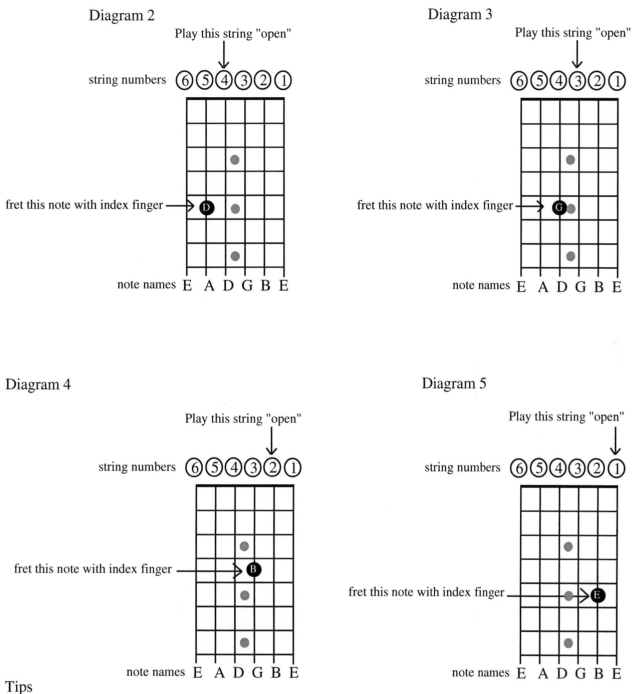

Diagram 2

Play this string "open"

string numbers ⑥⑤④③②①

fret this note with index finger → Ⓓ

note names E A D G B E

Diagram 3

Play this string "open"

string numbers ⑥⑤④③②①

fret this note with index finger → Ⓖ

note names E A D G B E

Diagram 4

Play this string "open"

string numbers ⑥⑤④③②①

fret this note with index finger → Ⓑ

note names E A D G B E

Diagram 5

Play this string "open"

string numbers ⑥⑤④③②①

fret this note with index finger → Ⓔ

note names E A D G B E

Tips

You should always try to tune each string by raising the string's pitch up to the correct note rather than lowering the pitch down into the correct note. It's not the end of the world if you don't do this but it usually helps to keep the guitar in tune. Also if you have just put new strings on your guitar you will need to "stretch the string out" so it stays more consistently in tune. This is done by first tuning your guitar so that all your strings are to their correct pitches and then gently pulling on each string to stretch it. This is done by pulling each string up and away from the guitar. After each "pulling" you will find that the string has gone flat. Tune the string back up to the correct pitch and continue this until you can pull gently on the each string and that string stays in tune. Do this to all 6 strings. This is a technique which is used by professionals to work around the problem that comes with changing strings. If you don't do this process you will find that you will constantly have to retune your guitar for the first couple of days after replacing the strings. If you use this method you will find that your guitar stays in tune much better.

7

Notes found on the Guitar

Below is a diagram showing you all the notes found on the guitar up to the 12th fret of each string. Some notes have two possible names. This is called its enharmonic spelling and is explained in the theory section found on the next few pages.

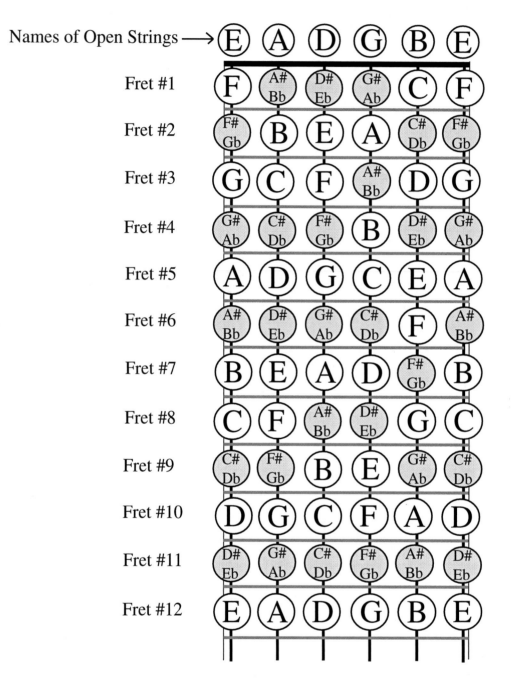

It is important that you learn all these notes overtime, but also remember it is important to understand the basics of music theory so you understand why these notes exist and how they relate to one another. The next section of this book will introduce you to basic music theory concepts. It is highly recommended that you read and reread these pages until this information is understood. You don't have to master all the music theory information before starting to learn the chords and chord progressions. Work back and forth until you can play the chords and chord progressions and reread the music theory section until its different components make sense to you.

Music Theory

The first thing a student must tackle to understand music theory is reading music notation. A detailed history of music notation is beyond the scope of this book and some inconsistencies have stayed in the course of its development. For the beginner these inconsistencies can be very confusing but inconsistent as it may be, music notation does have a standard for expressing itself visually and by understanding this system a whole new world of music is open to you.

In this system a series of lines and spaces are employed to create a visual representation of sound. Each line and space corresponds to a pitch. Each pitch is given a name A, B, C, D, E, F, or G. A clef sign is also used to designate what names each line and space will receive. The reason for the many types of clefs will be explained momentarily. First let us look at the treble clef. The treble clef places the note sequence in the order listed below. This complete system of lines and spaces with a clef sign is called a staff.

Example 1

As can be seen in example 1, each line and space corresponds to a different tone. If you want to have pitches higher or lower than the 5 lines and four spaces you can extend the staff by using ledger lines. Ledger lines give you the ability to represent higher and lower pitches by extending the staff. These extended pitches are called ledger line notes. (See example 2.)

Example 2

If we continue with this procedure we run into trouble as can be seen from the example below. When excessive ledger lines are used, reading music becomes very difficult. To alleviate this problem other clefs are employed to make reading these notes that are out of the treble clef's range easier. The note in the example 3 would be found in the bass or F clef on the 2nd space. (See example 4.)

Example 3

Example 4

C note

The same C in bass clef

Example 5 shows where the notes fall in the bass clef. We will only use the treble clef in this book but a basic understanding of the bass clef is important.

Example 5

If we look at our treble clef again we notice that there is an "e" on the first line and a "e" on the 4th space. Our ear recognizes these pitches as being the same pitch but the "e" on the 4th space sounds like a higher version of the low "e". In musical terminology the higher "e" is said to sound an octave higher than the lower "e". If we play these two "e's" on the guitar it would be the 2nd fret on the D string and fifth fret on the B string.

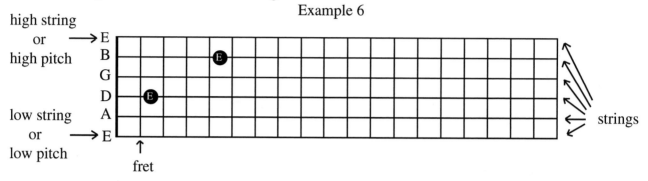

Example 6

high string
  or   → E
high pitch B
            G
            D
low string A
  or   → E
low pitch
          fret

To summarize what we have learned so far: there are 7 pitches which are represented on a staff with the letter names A,B,C,D,E,F,G. These 7 pitches keep repeating themselves in different octaves. To represent these notes in other octaves we need to use ledger lines or other clefs.

One of the inconsistencies of the notation system we have learned so far is that it doesn't show all the available notes in western music. There are a total of 12 pitches used in western music which of course as we have learned can be found in many different octaves. To show all 12 notes in the system, "sharp"(#) and "flat" (b) symbols are used to represent the tones that occur between the letter names of the notes.   For example between the note C and D there exists a pitch which can be called either C sharp or D flat. These notes are represented as follows C# or Db.   The (#) and (b) symbols work in the following way, the flat (b) lowers a pitch and a sharp (#) which raises the pitch. If a note is sharped it is said to have been raised a half step, if it is flatted it is said to have been lowered a half step. **A half step is the smallest distance possible in western music.** If we show all 12 notes on the staff within one octave we get what is called the chromatic scale. This scale contains all possible notes in the western system of music. Notice that there is no sharp or flat between E and F and B and C which is just one of those inconsistencies you have to accept with this notational system. Both chromatic scales shown below sound the same on the guitar; the decision to use sharps or flats depends on the musical situation. You will notice that the D in the chromatic scale with flats has a symbol in front of it. This symbol is called a natural sign. It is used to cancel the flat that appears before the previous D. **In written music, measures are used to delineate time, and sharps and flats carry through the whole measure until a new measure starts, unless a natural symbol is used to cancel it.**

Example 7   **Chromatic Scale**

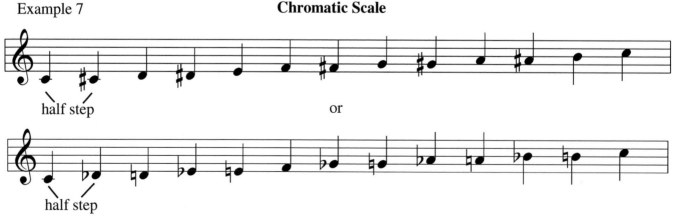

half step   or

half step

The 12 note chromatic scale can be represented in either of the two examples listed above. Remember a C# is the same note as a Db on the guitar. If you play on only one string of the guitar and move consecutively up each fret you will be playing a chromatic scale. If you were to play the above two examples of a chromatic scale you would start on the A string 3rd fret and move up each fret until you reach the 15th fret to complete the chromatic scale.

Example 8

Guitar Fretboard

Though the chromatic scale represents all 12 notes, much of western music of the last few centuries has been based around only 7 tones. If we extract these 7 notes as shown below we end up with a major scale.

Example 9   **Major scale derived from Chromatic scale**

Chromatic Scale

Major Scale

If we look at the distance in half steps between the notes of a major scale we see a pattern; whole, whole, half, whole, whole, whole, half. **All major scales are based on these intervals.**

Example 10   **C Major Scale**

11

If we apply this to the guitar fretboard the information works out accordingly: start on any note on the guitar and move up on one string starting with a whole step (2 frets), whole step, half step (1 fret), whole step, whole step, whole step, half step. This is one way to play a major scale on the guitar.

Guitar Fretboard

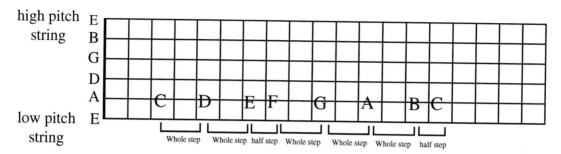

With this information you could play any major scale by following the pattern of whole step, whole step, half step, whole step, whole step, whole step, half step. The example below shows a D major scale.

Guitar Fretboard

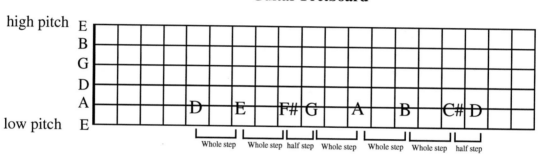

The notes of a C major scale C, D, E, F, G, A, B are commonly referred to as the diatonic notes of the key of C major. If we had the key of D major the diatonic notes would be D, E, F#, G, A, B, C#

If we use the major scale formula (1,1,1/2,1,1,1,1/2) we can figure out every major scale. We will find that each key has a different number of sharps or flats. If a piece of music uses a particular key, it's key signature is placed at the beginning of the piece of music. The following is a list of all the sharps and flats found in various keys. These are commonly referred to as the key signatures, and they occur after the clef sign and at the beginning of each line of music. The following key signatures are presented using a cycle 5 progression, which will be discussed on page 28.

Whole steps and half steps are the basic building blocks for the major scale. The whole step equals two half steps. The distance between two notes is called an interval. For example the distance between C and D is a whole step. This is also called a major second interval. It is important to know intervals because chords are frequently named for the intervals in their internal structure. All two note interval combinations from the root of the major scale are listed below.

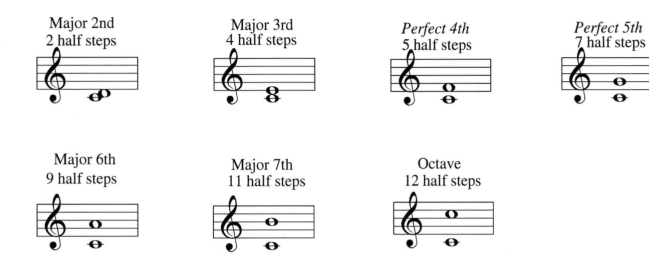

If we sharp any of these intervals we create an augmented interval. If we flat a major second, third, sixth or seventh we create a minor interval. If we flat a perfect fourth, a fifth, or an octave we get a diminished interval, and *if we double flat the major 7th we have a diminished 7th.* The following is a list of some of the more common augmented, minor and diminished intervals found in music.

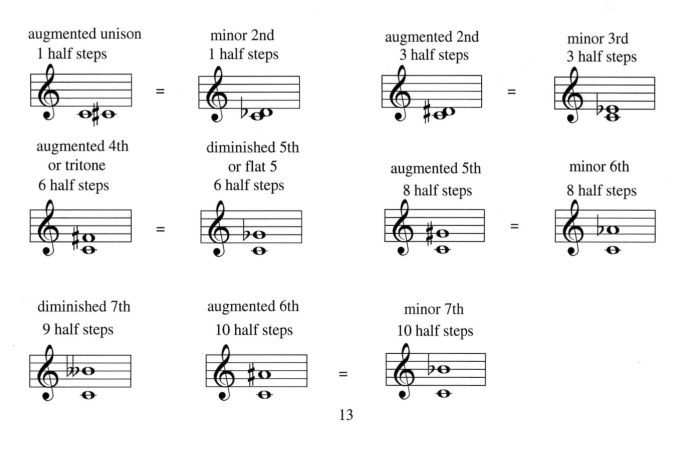

13

If we continue past the octave, intervals are given new names to show that they are more than an octave apart. Here are a few examples.

An augmented interval may be written in different ways. A (+) may appear before the number, or a (#) or (aug). If the interval is flatted it is usually indicated with a flat. Here are some of the common interval names you will need to know.

This knowledge of the chromatic scale, major scale and the construction of intervals is a valuable tool for understanding the internal structure of chords. Usually it takes a student around a year of study to remember all this information. For now do your best to start to learn and apply this information. If you feel that you would like to have another book to help you memorize all this music theory information I would recommend the Music Theory Workbook for Guitar Volume One ISBN 0964863243. This book covers all of the material presented here, but has a much broader scope and goes into greater detail. It also provides many exercises which help to ingrain the information, making it an excellent learning tool.

So far we have discussed 2 note intervals, sometimes called diads. When we add one more note to our 2 note interval we create a chord. A chord can be a combination of any 3 or more notes played at the same time. Western music builds chords using a wide variety of intervals. One of the most common ways to build chords is to stack up diatonic 3rd intervals. For example if we took C in the key of C and stacked up 3rds we would get C, E, and G because all of those notes are in the key of C and are a 3rd apart. **These structures built in thirds are commonly referred to as triads and the C note is said to be the root of the chord**.

C Major Triad

If we continue this process and build up diatonic triads above all the notes of C major we get the following 3 note structures:

Triads derived from stacking 3rds above a C major scale

These seven chords have a specific internal structure. The first structure C, E, and G form what is called a major chord. If we measure the distance or interval between each note using our chromatic scale we can find the formula for building major chords. Between C and E is 4 half steps or a major third. Between E and G is 3 half steps or a minor third. Therefore to create a major chord we need to combine a major third on the bottom and a minor third on the top. You will notice that the chords starting on F and on G are also major chords.

C major chord

minor 3rd
3 half steps

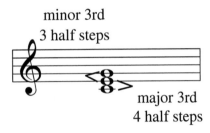
major 3rd
4 half steps

The second structure D, F, and A form what is called a minor chord, using the chromatic scale. Once again we can find the formula for building minor chords. Between D and F is 3 half steps or a minor third. Between F and A is 4 half steps or a major third. Therefore to create a minor chord we need to combine a minor third on the bottom and a major third on the top. You will notice that the chords starting on E and on A are also minor chords.

D minor chord

major 3rd
4 half steps
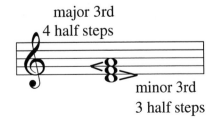
minor 3rd
3 half steps

15

This leaves us with one last structure; B, D, F which forms what is called a diminished chord. We won't be using this chord in this book but we should at least touch on it so we can complete the process. Using the same method we find that the distance between B and D is 3 half steps or a minor third. Between D and F is 3 half steps or a minor third. Therefore to create a diminished chord we need to combine a minor third on the bottom and a minor third on the top.

B diminished chord

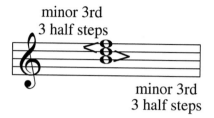

Below is a list of all the triads and their chord names. These chords are referred to as the diatonic triad or chords of a major key. You will see each of these chords labeled in many ways. C major could be shown as: C major, CMaj, C, CM. D minor could be shown as: D minor, Dmin, D-, Dm. B diminished could be shown as: B diminished, B dim, or B°.

They are also numbered sequentially which allows someone to refer to the D minor chord in the key of C, as a "II chord". Because many contemporary tunes are written using only the diatonic chords of a key it is a very common practice among musicians to learn the diatonic chords of every key using numbers and letters to aid in the memorization and quick learning of new songs.

Diatonic chords of C Major

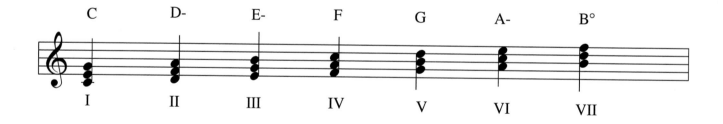

At this point many students wonder why all this information is so important. Let me give you one quick example. If you have followed this whole theory discussion up to this point you now know how most songs are written. If you were to write a song in C major, 90 per cent of the time you would only use the diatonic chords of the key of C. Therefore learning the diatonic chords of each key helps you to write music and also to understand why certain chords are used in your favorite tunes. Try analyzing some of the progressions found in the back of this book. Most of them only use the diatonic chords of a key.

This completes our theory discussion. There are many more chord types that are used in music and if you would like to understand and to increase your knowledge of these chords I would once again recommend the Music Theory Workbook for Guitar Volume One ISBN 0964863243.

As each chord is introduced in this book the chord tones will be shown in staff notation along with a list of the notes contained in the chord. Remember that memorizing the notes contained in each chord presented, along with knowing what notes you are playing will open up a whole new world on the guitar. The example below shows how each chord type will appear.

Chord tones for a C major chord

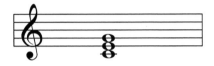

It is beyond the scope of this book to present all the chords possible in music. There is one other chord though, that we will be using that we should have a short discussion about. To first recap a little, the notes of each chord are called the chord tones. For example, the chord tones of a C major chord are C, E, and G. But, It is also possible to build chords that contain more notes. The next most common chord type found in music is a four note structure which is commonly referred to as a 7th chord. To build a 7th chord you add a note a third above the triads we have just discussed. If we add a minor third above our C major triad we get C, E, G, Bb

This new structure C, E, G and Bb forms a dominant 7th chord. Using the chromatic scale we can find the formula for building dominant 7th chords. Between C and E is 4 half steps or a major third, between E and G is 3 half steps or a minor third, between G and Bb is 3 half steps or a minor third. **Therefore to create a dominant 7th chord we need to combine a major third on the bottom and a minor third in the middle and a minor third on the top**.

Dominant 7th Chord
1,3,5,b7

When you hear a dominant seventh chord, you will realize that it too, has been used in many of your favorite songs as a way to enhance the harmonic passages of a composition. The dominant has a special characteristic in that it feels like it wants to resolve. Understanding these tendencies can greatly aid you in applying this chord. If you would like a more detailed explanation of why this is, check out the Chord Workbook for Guitar Volume One ISBN 0964863219

The guitar only has 6 possible notes it can play at once so sometimes certain notes are left out of a chord to make it playable. At other times notes will be doubled to make a fuller sound. You will also notice in many places that certain chord tones have been omitted to make the chord easier to play.

As can be seen from the example 1 below, we start with our basic C major chord. It is combined into a chord on the guitar which is both playable and has a good sound. In example 2 we have the root, 5th, root, 3rd. **The combination of notes that form the chord is called the chord voicing.** The tablature in example 3 then shows fret location with the circled number, the fingering with the number next to the dots, and an X placed above to indicate which string is not played. Sometimes open circles will indicate that open strings are to be played (see page example 3 below). Index finger is 1, middle finger is 2, ring finger 3, little finger is 4.

Example 1   Example 2

C major   **Chord voicing on guitar**

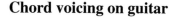
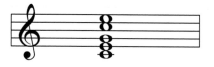

Example 3

C

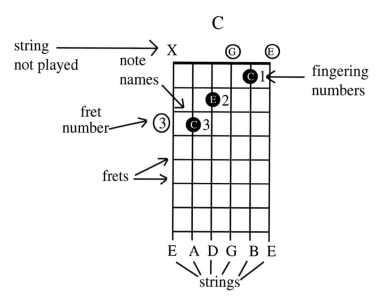

Introduction to Chord Voicings

If by chance you haven't yet learned the chords found in this book, I recommend you first spend a few days forming and playing each chord. Remember it will take a few weeks if not a month before your fingers develop calluses so you may experience a little pain. This pain can be minimized by pressing on the string only hard enough to make the note sound. Most students that are beginners usually press on the notes a lot harder than they need to, and therefore experience pain or fatigue after playing only for a short while. I recommend if you are a total beginner to play in five or ten minute intervals with 20 minute rest periods. This will help your hand to acclimate to the guitar. It will also help you to know when you have practiced enough because during your 20 minute rest intervals you will feel how fatigued your hand really is.

There are two types of chords found in this book; "open" and "barre." "Open" refers to the fact that you are playing some open strings when you play each chord. "Barre" refers to the fact that you lay your first finger across multiple strings in order to create chords that can be moved around to different areas of the guitar neck to play the same chord at different pitches.

These two types of chords are the ones most used when the guitar is played as a solo accompaniment, especially in folk and rock. There are of course many other ways to play chords on the guitar. Depending on the style and function of the guitar within a group, different chord voicings are called upon to fill these situations. For example when a guitar is playing with a funk band you would use a completely different set of chords than the chords found in this book.

There are many ways you could work through this book. You could just start with each chord and learn a few each week. For some students this works fine, while others need to apply each chord they learn to music, so it makes sense to them. If you are of the latter category, I would suggest looking first at the chords used in the chord progression on page 37. Follow the directions on page 36 to help you learn the chord progressions.

This book only contains the basic chords commonly found in folk and rock. When you are ready to move on to other chords and progressions, check page 49 for suggestions on further study. I have also made reference to other books along the way that can help you with specific topics.

Root Position Major Chords

Possible chord tones for major
1,3,5

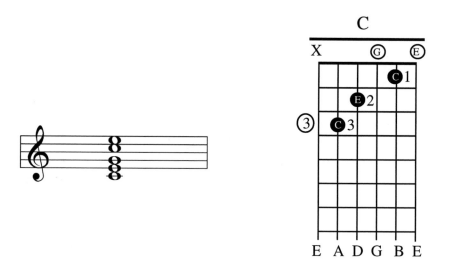

The C chord is usually one of the easier chords to play. It is common that a beginning student will have a problem keeping the 2nd finger curved enough to allow the "open" G string to sound. It is also common to have the same problem with the "open" high E string.

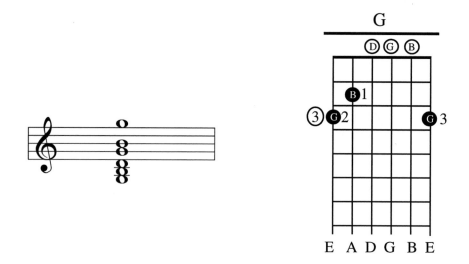

The G chord is usually one of the easier chords for a beginner but it is sometimes hard to change to it quickly in a chord progression. Make sure your "open" D, G and B strings ring out clearly.

Root Position Major Chords Continued
Possible chord tones for major
1,3,5

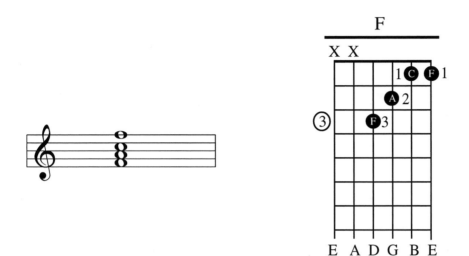

The F chord is usually quite difficult for a beginner. The main problem comes with placing your 1st finger across two strings at once while at the same time reaching the F and A notes with your 2nd and 3rd fingers. (See photo 13) Give yourself a good couple of weeks with this chord. With the F chord and any chord you have problems with, practicing it many times a day for a few short moments will go a long way toward mastering the chord. Don't worry if it sounds good, just finger the chord and play it. Over time your fingers will gain strength and agility.

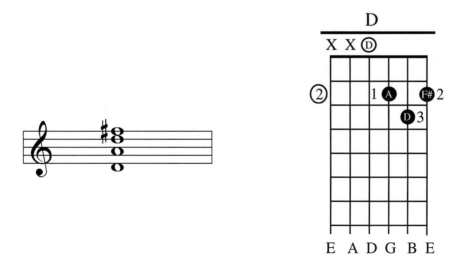

This is one of the easiest chords on the guitar. Watch out when strumming the chord that you only play the top 4 strings. You will sometimes hear people strumming the open A string with this chord. This will all depend on whether it works with the song in question.

Root Position Major Chords Continued
Possible chord tones for major
1,3,5

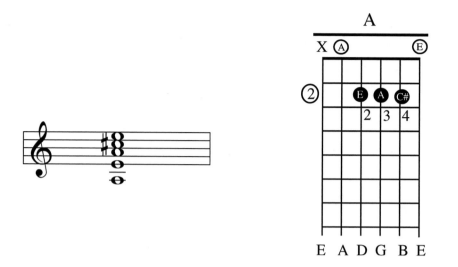

This chord can also be fingered with your 1st, 2nd, and 3rd finger where your 1st finger would be on the E on the D strings, 2nd finger on the A on the G string and your 3rd finger on the C# on the B string.

If you would like to apply some of the chords you have learned so far give it a try. There are now two chord progression you can play with the chords presented (See pages 38 or 41.) You should first check page 43 for directions on how to practice the chord progressions. If you have problems with the rhythm in the chord progressions, see pages 32-35.

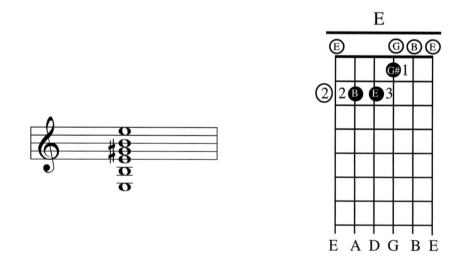

This is yet another easy chord on the guitar and by strumming all 6 strings you get a nice big sound on your guitar. Everyone loves "E!"

Root Position Minor Chords

Possible chord tones for minor
1,b3,5

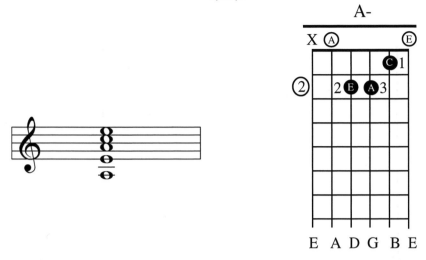

There are now three more chord progressions you can play with the chords learned so far. See pages 37, 39, and 40. You should first check page 43 for directions for how to practice the chord progressions. If you have problems with the rhythm in the chord progressions see pages 32-35.

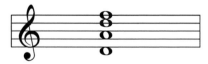

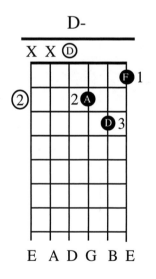

Root Position Minor Chords

Possible chord tones for minor
1,b3,5

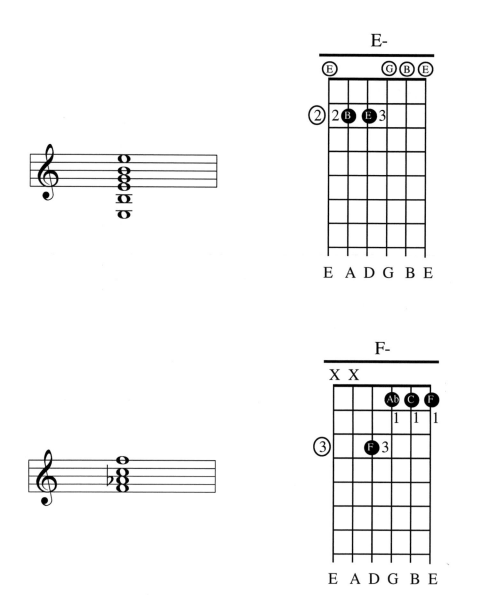

E-

E   G B E

② 2 B E 3

E A D G B E

F-

X X

Ab C F
1 1 1

③ F 3

E A D G B E

    F minor presents the same problem that F major did. It is hard to place your 1st finger across three strings and then get your 3rd finger up to the F on the 3rd fret. I sometimes recommend playing this chord higher up on the guitar neck. The frets are closer together as you move up the neck so the stretch is not as difficult. Over time, you should practice moving the chord down until you can play it as indicated. Although the F minor chord isn't used in any of the chord progressions found in this book it is an important stepping stone to playing the "barre" chords starting on page 27. See photo 13 for a close look at playing the F minor chord.

Root Position Dominant 7th Chords
Possible chord tones for 7
1,3,5,b7

C7

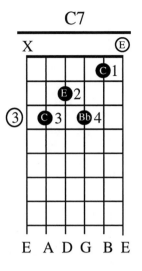

E A D G B E

D7

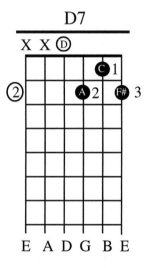

E A D G B E

E7

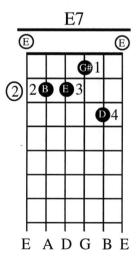

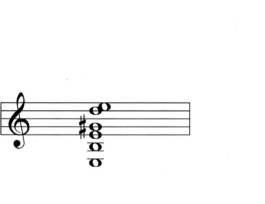

E A D G B E

Dominant chords are commonly used in a Blues progression.   See page 47-8 for an example.

Root Position Dominant 7th Chords
Possible chord tones for 7
1,3,5,b7

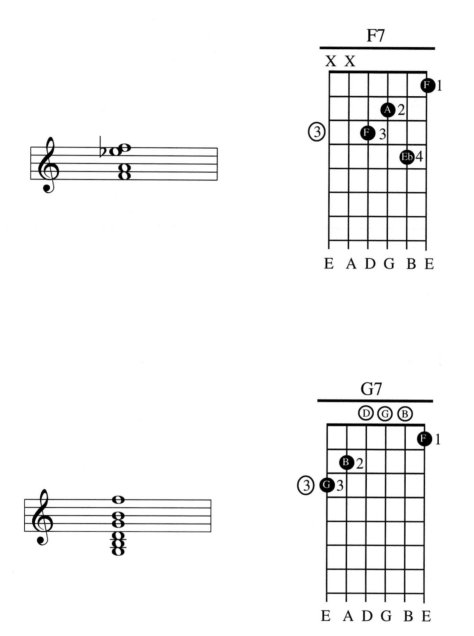

Be careful when playing the G7 chord that all the "open" strings sound clear. Although neither of these chords are present in any of the chord progressions starting on page 39 they both are commonly found in popular tunes.

Barre Chords

The next chords we will look at are the "Barre Chords" (pronounced "bar".) These chords are the same chords as we have already learned but we are now playing them in a different way. As previously discussed there is more than one way to play any chord by doubling or leaving out certain notes.

These barre chords are some of the most commonly played chord voicings on the guitar. In general you will find that the "open" voiced chords you have just learned are used more in folk music while the barre chords are found more in rock.

Barre chords are not easy for a beginner (see picture 14.) It takes time to develop strength in your index finger to hold down more that one string at a time. You will find the practice suggestion on the next page to be a great way to learn these barre chords. The cool thing about these chords is that you can slide them around the neck to play other chords of the same type. When you start to practice these chords don't worry so much about how they sound just form the chord and play it. Over time the chords will start to sound better as your hand is able to play each note clearly. If you find these chords to be quite difficult and frustrating I recommend you play a barre chord and then play each string and adjust your hand to make each note sound. You will probably find you are unable to make all the notes sound clearly together but if you use the technique of playing each note and adjusting your hand you will find eventually the barre chord starts sounding better and better.

I can't over emphasize the importance of practicing the barre chords using the technique on the next page. Barre chords allow you to play one fingering pattern and then move it around the neck to play all the possible types of that chord. For instance once your learn the major chord presented on the next page you can move this voicing around the neck to play ANY major chord. You just need to memorize what the "root note" or bottom note of the chord is and instantly you have learned all the major chords. This is one of the great things about a guitar. It allows you to move barre chords around to different frets so that you can play all possible chords.

Give yourself a few weeks if not a month on these chords. They are very hard on your hand at first and require time for your hand to adjust. The chord progressions in the back of this book will also help you to apply and develop these chords until they sound clear and distinct.

Leaving out notes in chords

It is common to leave out certain notes of a chord when playing barre chords but you will also find this happening with other chords as you explore music more in-depth. There is an hierarchy of which notes are left out more often.

The 5th of a chord is the first note to be left out. This is because it is the note that least defines the sound of any chord. The (1) or the root is the next to go. This is because usually the bass player in a group is playing the root so you don't need to double it.

Adding notes to chords

It is also common to add notes to chords. It is beyond to scope of this book to explain all the theory and occurrences of this phenomenon. Added notes can create a great effect in music, giving the chords inner life and movement. So that you have a general idea of the process of adding notes here is a very cursory explanation. The notes that are most commonly added are the passing tones of the scale that is used for the chord you are playing. Another process that is also used is the addition of the available tensions for any chord. Both processes overlap each other and can add great color and movement for your chord progressions.. If you would like to explore this more I recommend Chord Workbook for Guitar Volume One. ISBN 0964863219.

Moveable Chord Forms

The chords that follow allow you to learn a chord form and then move it around the neck to get that chord type for every degree of a chromatic scale. All the notated examples of chords should be practiced "cycle 5". Cycle 5 is a way to play all 12 chromatic notes by moving in a pattern of 5ths (or 7 half steps) down from the previous chord. Therefore C moves to F, then Bb, Eb, Ab, Db, Gb, B, E, A, D, G. On the guitar this means you would play for example the first C major chord at the 3rd fret as indicated and then play the same fingering at the 8th fret on the 5th string and you get F major, then the 1st fret for Bb major, 6th fret for Eb major etc. The example below shows you how to proceed.

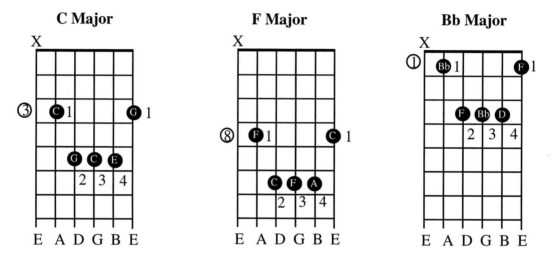

Don't just memorize the position of each of these chords without thinking of what chord you are playing. Memorize the shape so you can recognize the chord type, then memorize the bottom of each chord to tell you which chord you are playing as you move through the cycle 5 progression. Remember all examples in this book have the root as the lowest note of each chord voicing so by memorizing the bottom note as you move cycle 5 you will be memorizing the notes on the E and A strings. When you have memorized the notes on the E and A strings you only need to memorize the new chord type as you move through this book.

Cycle 5 is one of the most common chord movements in music. Therefore practicing chords cycle 5 is excellent preparation for playing music.

Cycle 5 Progression or the Circle of Fifths

C, F, Bb, Eb, Ab, Db, Gb, B, E, A, D, G

It is also a good idea to go through the cycle in a couple of ways. For example when you get to Gb think F# instead. Gb and F# are said to be enharmonic keys because their pitches are the same on the guitar but their names are different. Refer back to your list of keys to find other enharmonic keys to practice.

Try not to count down a certain number of frets to find the next chord. Memorizing the pitches of each fret will be much better in the long run. All moveable chord form found in this book should be practiced using the cycle 5 movement, and remember when practicing always think what note you are playing rather than memorizing the position.

Root Position Major Chords

Possible chord tones for C major

1,3,5

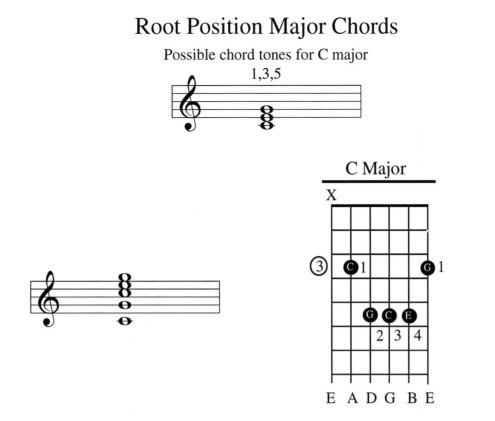

C Major

It is also possible to finger this chord by replacing your 2nd, 3rd, and 4th finger with your 3rd finger and pressing down across the aforementioned notes. This requires flexibility in the 1st joint of your **3rd** finger. Photo 11 shows this flexibility using the 1st finger for demonstration.

With the C major barre chord and a working knowledge of how to play it in any key (which is found on page 28 (you can now check out the chord progression on page 44.) You should first check page 43 for directions for how to practice the chord progressions. If you have problems with the rhythm in the chord progressions see pages 32-35.

Please note: Your first finger essentially presses down all the way across the neck, but your 2nd, 3rd and 4th fingers are creating higher notes on the A, D and G strings.

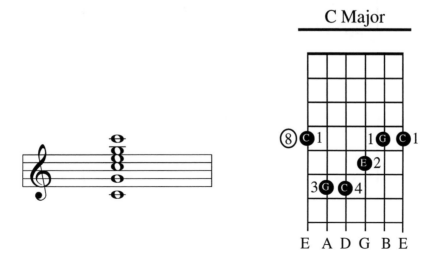

C Major

This is one of the most popular barre chords. Make sure to play this chord through the exercises on page 28. This will help you to memorize all the notes on the low E string and prepare you for the chord progression found on page 46. See photo 14 for a close up look at this chord.

29

Root Position Minor Chords

Possible chord tones for C-
1,b3,5

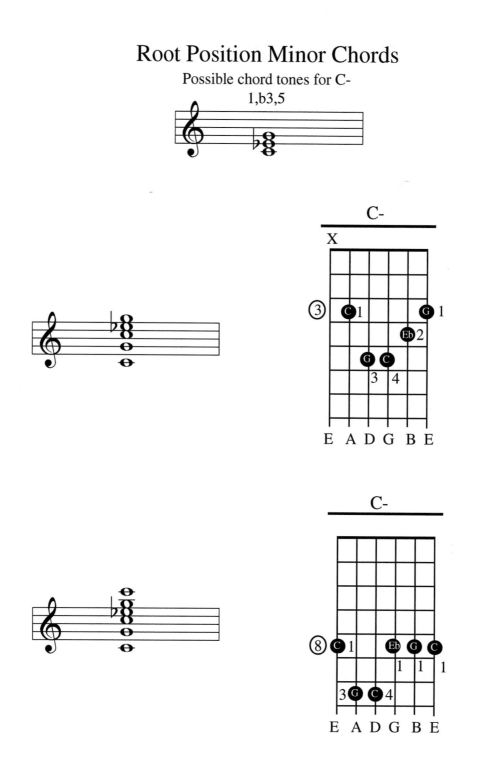

Once again play these chords through the exercise found on page 28. After you feel like you know the minor chords in all keys, try the chord progressions on pages 42 and 43. You should first check page 43 for directions for how to practice the chord progressions. If you have problems with the rhythm in the chord progressions see pages 32-35.

Congratulations for making it this far!

Believe it or not you have now learned most of the chords you will commonly find in rock and folk. Although we still have a few more chords to learn your palette of chord possibilities is now at a point that you should be able to buy books by your favorite artists and feel familiar with most of the chords.

Root Position Dominant 7th Chords

Possible chord tones for C7

1,3,5,b7

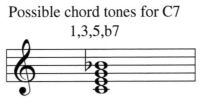

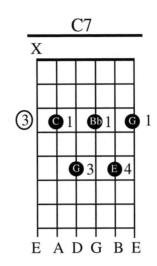

Make sure the G string sounds with this chord to give it the proper sound.

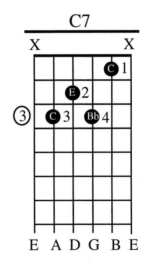

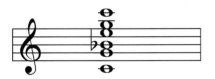

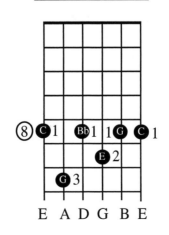

Make sure the D string sounds with this chord to give it the proper sound. You should play these chords once again through the exercise on page 28. You can then play the blues chord progression found on page 47 and 48.

31

Understanding Rhythm

One of the most overlooked aspects of learning to play an instrument is rhythm. You can learn all the chords in the world, play all the scales, and understand all the theory, but if you don't have a basic understanding of rhythm none of it will sound like music. Rhythm is the heart beat of music and you need to understand it at least at a rudimentary level in order to play any piece of music.

The following pages will present you with a simple discussion of how rhythm is notated in music. This will help you a lot in understanding the rhythms in the chord progression but will also help you with any piece of music you come across. Audio examples in the form of midifiles are available on the muse-eek.com website, so you can hear what each rhythm sounds like. Each file will give you a on bar count off (4 ticks) and then play the example. Using these help files will great speed up your understanding of rhythm.

The Nuts and Bolts of Rhythm

The rhythm in a piece of music is presented in overall units call "measures" These measures are further divided up into beats. (More on this in a moment) Example One shows you one "measure" of music. There are many different symbols in a measure of music. These symbols show how to play the music. To the far left there is always a clef sign. This tells the reader what pitch level the notes will be on the staff. The clef sign used here is the treble clef sign, therefore the 4 notes presented in this measure would be four C's. The next symbol is the time signature. This tells you how the measure will be divided rhythmically. In this case the time signature is 4/4. The top 4 tells you how many beats are in a measure. In this case the measure has 4 beats in it. The bottom 4 tells you what unit of measure will be used to show those 4 beats. In this case the 4 represents a quarter note. So this whole measure is divided up into 4 quarters and these 4 quarters are each represented by a note called a quarter note. A quarter note would be held for one beat. A line is placed at the end of each measure to show where the end of each measure is.

Example 1

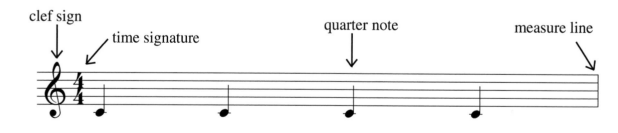

You can use the suggested midifiles to play any of the examples found here or you can use a metronome to help you maintain a steady pulse. A metronome plays a steady clicking sound at a user selectable rate. This can help you maintain a steady pulse as you work on the exercises. Metronomes can be purchased at any music store but you also can find many electronic metronomes on the internet that will work on your computer.

Rhythm can of course be much more or less complicated than example 1. In example 2 we still have a 4/4 measure and it still has only 4 beats in the measure but we have only one note which happens on beat one. This note takes up all four beats of the measure so you would sustain the sound for four beats. This note is called a whole note. Example 3 shows a measure that has been divided up into two equal parts. These notes are called half notes and because we have a 4/4 measure there can only be 2 half notes in a measure because a half note gets 2 beats. The first note is played on beat one and the second note is played on beat 3.

Example 2   Example 3

As I have said, rhythm can be much more complicated than the previous example. In example 4 we still have a 4/4 measure and it still has only 4 beats in the measure but each beat has been divided into equal divisions to form a new rhythm. So now rather than just four rhythmic hits in the measure there are eight. These new notes are referred to as eighth notes because it takes 8 eighth notes to make up one measure of 4/4. So for each beat you would play two notes equally dividing that beat into two parts.

Example 4

Rhythm can get even more complicated than these examples. We can also add in rest periods where you don't play anything. The next page will explain this process and how it is notated.

Rests

In each of the rhythms presented in the previous examples we could have left some notes out to create other rhythms. These left out notes are called rests and use the symbols shown in the examples below. During the rests you don't play anything. You will see in the forthcoming examples that when rests are placed into measures the rhythm can become quite complex. We will start with some simple examples.

Examples 5-7 show measures with three kinds of rests. In example 5 there is a whole note rest. Nothing would be played during this measure. Example 6 shows a half note rest. In this case nothing would be played for the first two beats of the measure. Example 7 shows a quarter note rest. In this case nothing would be played for beat 3 of this measure.

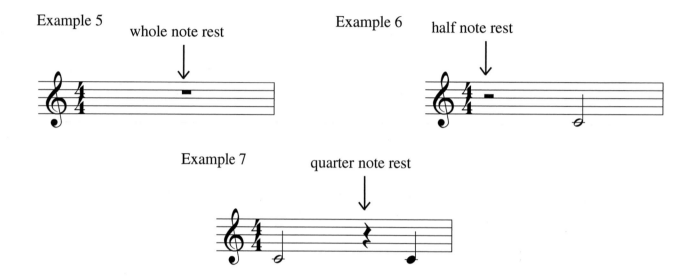

Examples 8 show a measure that is composed of eighth notes but in which one of the eighth notes has been left out.

Dots

A dot can be placed after a note or rest to lengthen its value. A dot adds 1/2 of the note's value, therefore in example 9, the dot placed after the quarter note adds a one eighth value so you hold this note for 3 eighths duration. (One quarter plus one eighth = 3 eighths) Example 10 shows the same situation but with a tie rather than a rest.

Example 9   Example 10

Ties

Ties can also be placed into music to lengthen a particular note. Example 11 shows two quarter notes tied together. Example 12 shows what this rhythm would sound like.

Example 11   Example 12

Although I don't recommend it as a long term habit, a beginner often needs a method to help count each beat and subdivision. Over time you should develop the ability to recognize any rhythm and know what it sounds like. But again, if you are a beginner or you are having a problem with a rhythm, counting is a way to work it through. The follow examples give the counting method I recommend.

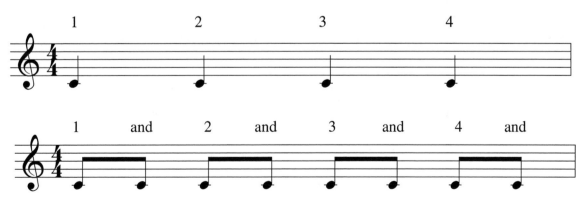

We have only discussed the rudimentary aspect of rhythm so that you can play the chord progressions starting on page 39. I highly recommend you spend more time developing your rhythm skills. Two books I would suggest are "Rhythm Primer" and "Understanding Rhythm." You will find a complete list of the titles in the "Rhythm Series" listed in the back of this book

Applying your new chords to common chord progressions

The following pages contain chord progressions that will help you to apply the chords and the rhythm knowledge you have learned so far. There are many ways to approach these chord progressions depending on your current level. There are 10 progressions in total. The first eight chord progressions have been divided up into 3 levels of difficulty. Each level gets progressively harder so that the total beginner can slowly master each aspect of changing chords, strumming and keeping time. The first level entitled "A" gives you just the chords with a simple strumming pattern. The second level "B" gives you the chord progression with a more complex strumming and rhythmic pattern. The third level entitled "C" gives you the actual way this progression would be played. By working your way through each level you should find that you progress quickly.

Many help files are available on the muse-eek.com website to enable a student to master each level and each progression. Again it's not essential to use these files to learn the progression but they can make the process a lot more fun, and also help to point out problems that you might not be aware of. Whether you use the files or not you should work on the progressions in the following manner.

How to Practice the Chord Progressions

1. Play each example (A, B, C) slowly, using a metronome or a help file, or count the correct number of beats for each.
2. Follow the picking directions (see bottom of page for explanation of picking symbols)
3. Speed up the example over a week of practice then proceed to the next level.

How to use the help files on muse-eek.com

You have two different types of files available to help you master each progression. The midifiles (played by downloading a midifile player from the muse-eek.com website) will play each example at whatever tempo you select. Start with Exercise A at a slow tempo and slowly speed up each progression until you can move from one chord to another quickly. When you feel you are ready, move on to Exercise B, and repeat the same process. When you move on to Exercise C you also can use an mp3 audio file of an actual guitar playing the progression.

This concept of using audio and midifiles can really speed up your progress on the guitar. I urge you to take the time to set up your computer so you can take advantage of these help files. You will also notice that the midifile player allows you to speed up and slow down the audio so you can gradually play the chords faster and faster.

I know it is hard to remember all the chords we have looked at so far. Chord progressions are a great tool to help you remember all the chord voicings. I have only suggested one group of chords for each chord progression but as you have learned there is more than one way to play each chord. (There are "open" voicings and "barre" chords.) After you have mastered these progressions try replacing the chords with alternate possibilities. This will help you to memorize more chords and give you more agility on the guitar. Remember to be patient with yourself. Some students can take months before this flows smoothly while others get it going within weeks. Don't dwell on what your inherent ability might be; just remember that perseverance pays off and is its own reward.

Explanation of Strumming Symbols

The following symbols are used to indicate an up or down stroke. (See video clip 9 for an example of strumming chord progression #3.)

⊓ = Strum with a downward motion

⋁ = Strum with an upward motion

Chord Progression 1

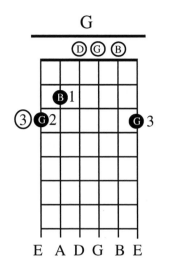
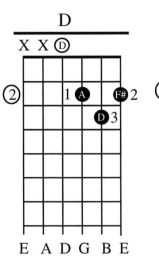
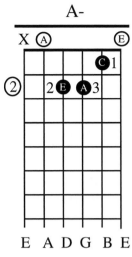

Example A

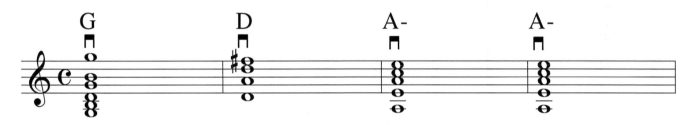

Example B

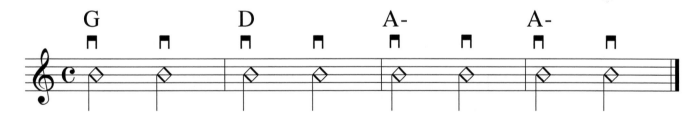

Example C

mm=112

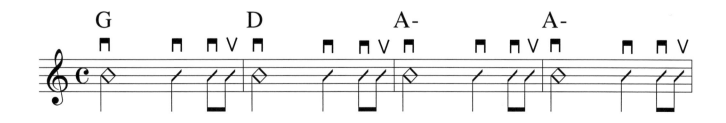

Chord Progression 2

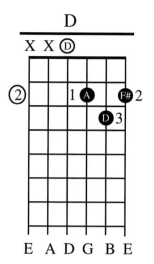

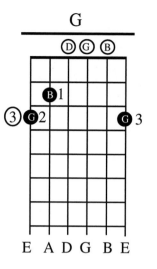

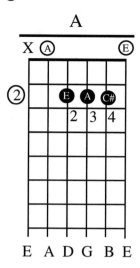

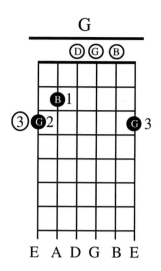

Example A

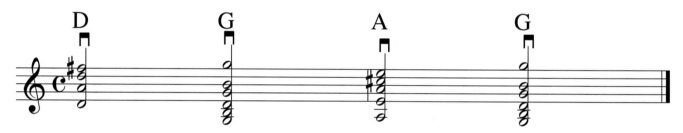

Example B

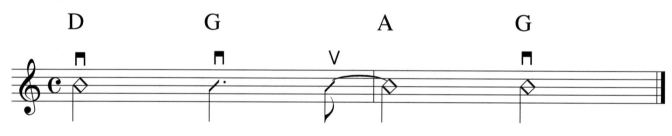

Example C

mm=120

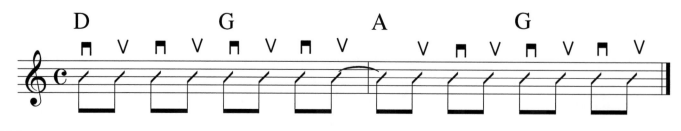

Chord Progression 3

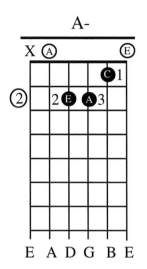
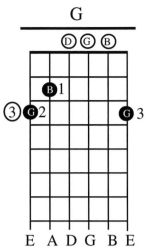
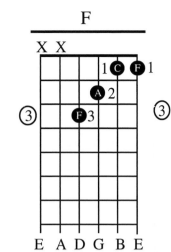
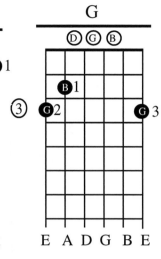

Example A

Example B

Example C

mm=88

Chord Progression 4

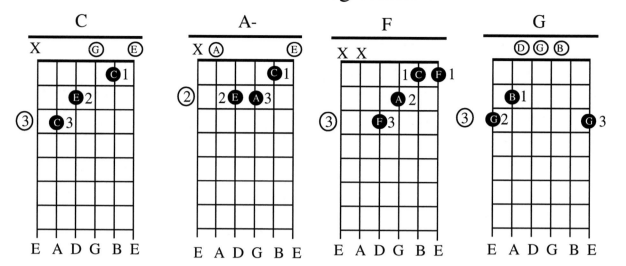

Example A

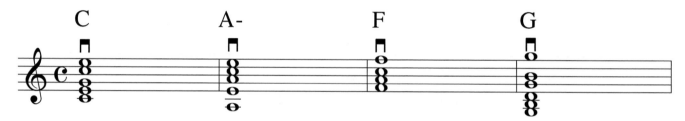

Example B

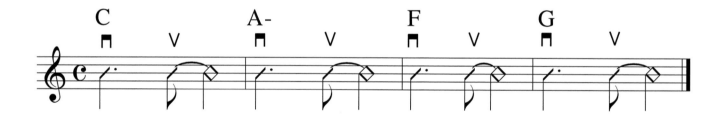

Example C

mm=88

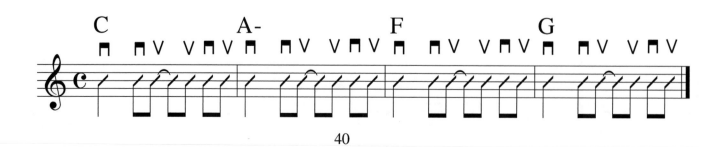

Chord Progression 5

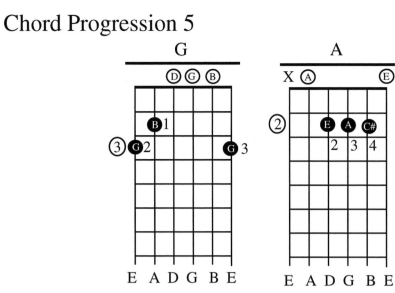

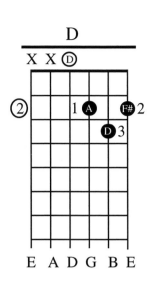

Example A

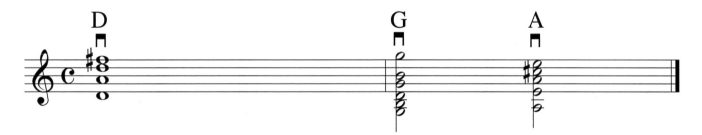

Example B

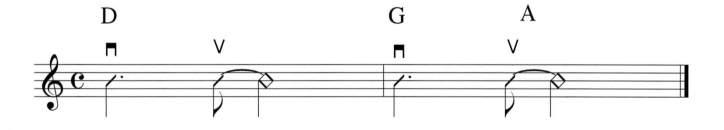

Example C

mm=100

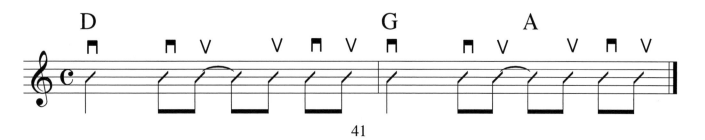

Chord Progression 6

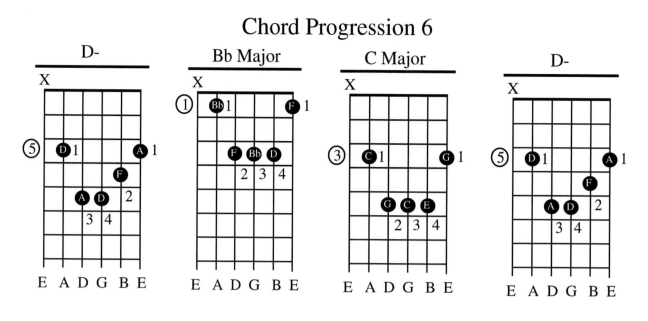

Example A

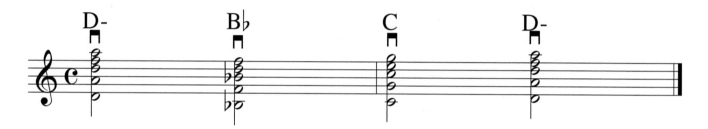

Example B

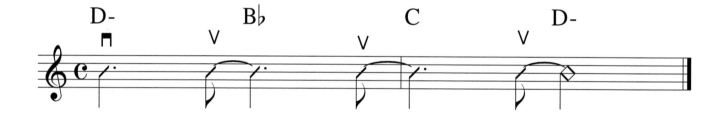

Example C

mm=104

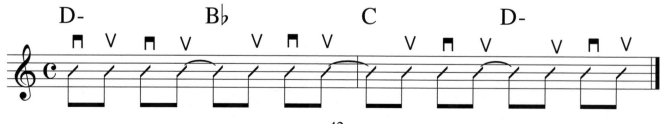

Chord Progression 7

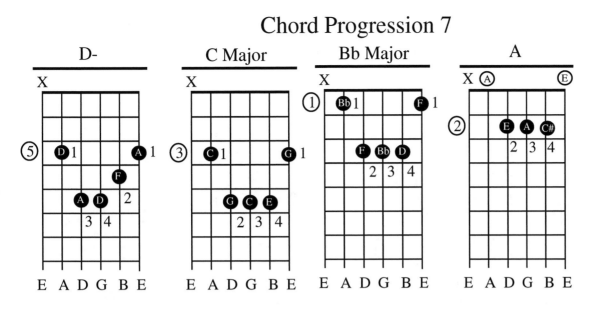

Example A

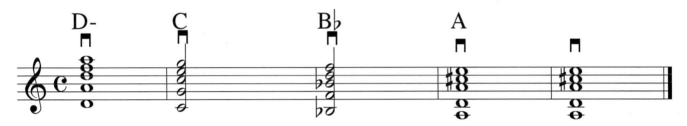

Example B

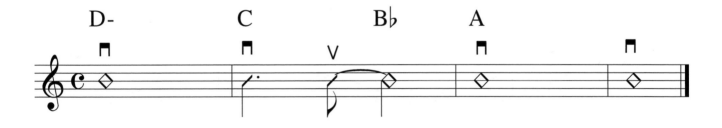

Example C

mm=112

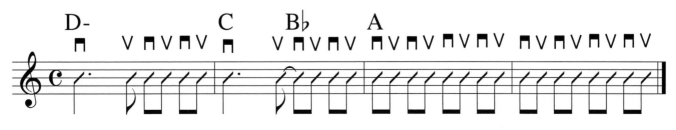

43

Chord Progression 8

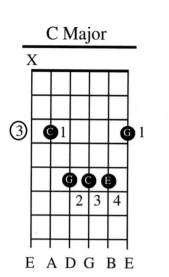

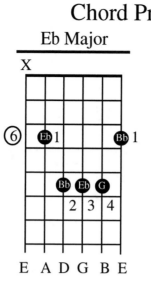

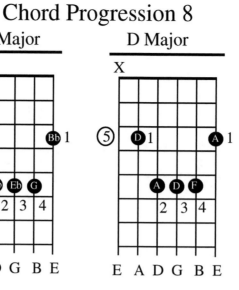

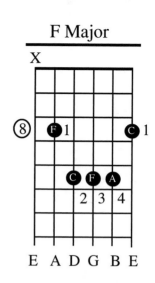

Example A

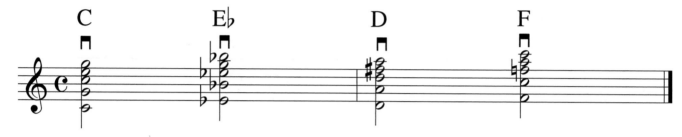

Example B

Example C

mm=100

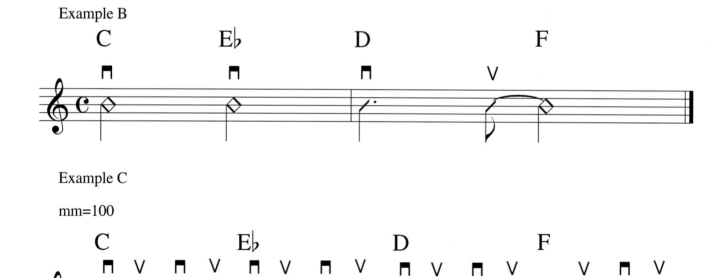

For this type of progression and style it is common to just play the bottom 3 notes of each chord. This style of playing only the bottom 3 notes of a major or minor barre chord is frequently referred to as playing "power chords." Distortion is also a key element in the effectiveness of the "power chord" style. Distortion can be achieved by either turning your amp and guitar up very loud or using a distortion box.

44

Chord Progression 9

This is our first 8 bar progression and our first using a dominant 7th chord. Work with this page until you can switch chords fluently and then try the progression with the rhythm found on the next page.

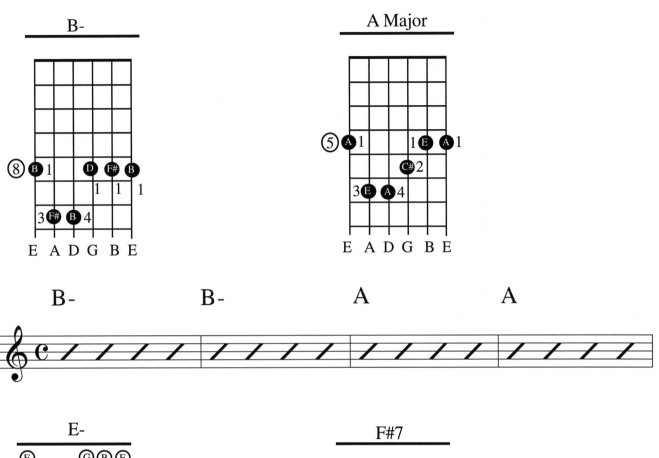

| B- | B- | A | A |

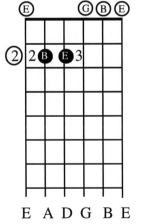
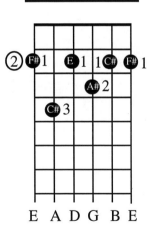

| E- | E- | F♯7 | F♯7 |

Chord Progression 9

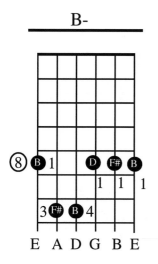

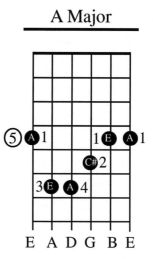

mm=160

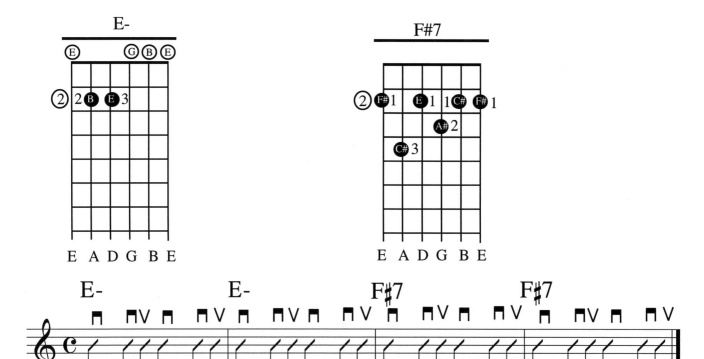

Chord Progression 10
The Blues

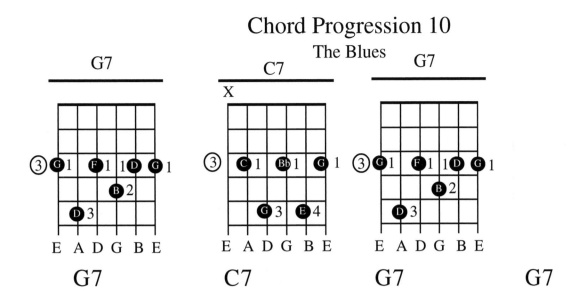

G7   C7   G7   G7

C7   C7   G7   G7

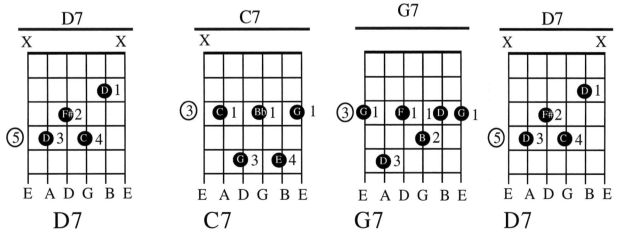

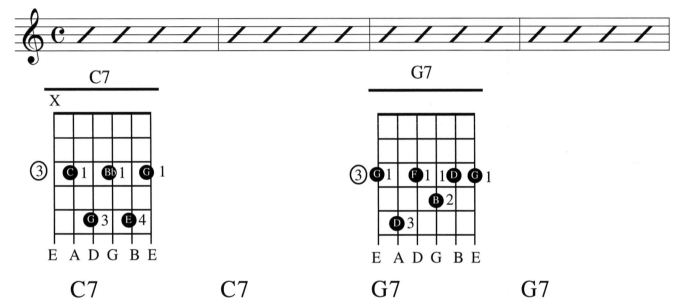

D7   C7   G7   D7

Chord Progression 10

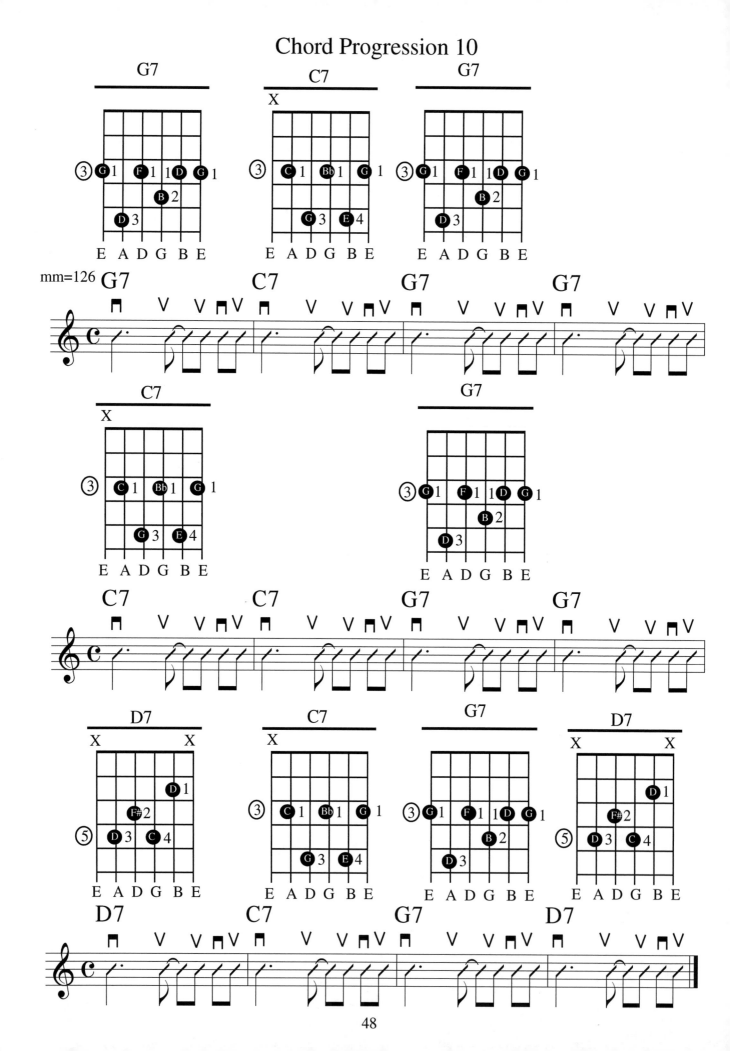

48

What's Next

This book only covers a few of the chords commonly used in traditional rock and folk, which is in turn only one small part of the larger picture of your development as a musician/guitarist. It is important to continue your exploration into the basics of music and music theory so you can have a better understanding of what you are actually doing with the music you are playing. For the guitar this is particularly true because many students just blindly learn chords and expect that this will be enough for them to build a musical ability on the guitar.

I frequently use the analogy of learning a new language when comparing the short sighted ideas people have about studying the guitar. For instance, if you were learning the English language, would you learn only those words which allow you to order a cup of coffee and say "thank you?" Of course not: you would want to understand the grammar of the language and the meaning of many words, so you could form your own sentences and communicate at least on a rudimentary level with an English speaking person. It is the same for music. You need to educate yourself to get a deeper understanding of the basic elements of music, so you will understand what you are playing. Then you can use the musical information you have learned to create other combinations. You will then be able to communicate your musical ideas to others effortlessly and *it's all about communicating isn't it?* Learning music on this deeper level is harder, but not as difficult as you might think. By using the right textbooks you can eventually educate yourself to a level where music makes sense both aurally and theoretically.

If this seems like a path you would like to follow, I would recommend purchasing two books to get started. "Chord Workbook for Guitar Volume One" and "Music Theory Workbook for Guitar Volume One." "Chord Workbook for Guitar Volume One" contains a music theory section written in simple language you can understand. The book continues with the chords you need to know as an evolving guitarist. It will also give you chord progressions to help you apply the new chords you have learned. "Music Theory Workbook for Guitar Volume One" explains the basics of music theory and gives you hundreds of exercises that you can work on to not only understand how chords are built but to see where these notes are on the guitar. Both these books give you a foundation that most students of music learn in their freshman year at college but is now available to you in book form. The methods found in these two books are the techniques used in music colleges throughout the world. By working through these books you too, can properly educate yourself.

Further Thoughts on Practicing and Playing Music

This book may have been your first contact with making music. It is therefore important to share some thoughts on how to think about the relationship of the creative process with the technical process of learning to play an instrument. I always tell my students there are two sides to playing music; one is <u>creative</u> and one is <u>technical</u>. For a beginning student it is very easy to lose track of one or the other. Student A will open this book and diligently work through all the exercises, learn the chords and chord progressions but find that their playing feels mechanical. On the other hand Student B will open this book to the first chord progression skipping all the information about technique, music theory, rhythm and learn to play it in a day or two and then just start creating new chord progressions by rearranging the chords, and trying new strumming patterns. Both approaches have their merits and their pitfalls. Student A has learned the necessary technical information but is not spending enough time just being creative with the information. Student B is all creativity but finds over time that their hand hurts, their ideas stagnate, and they don't understand basic musical concepts. The answer to this dilemma is to work on both sides of the equation. Be creative with the information you learn in this book. Experiment with different combinations of chords, rhythms, strumming patterns. On the other hand learn how to play correctly so you can take full advantage of your talents, learn your music theory so you understand how music is put together so you can notice patterns and possibilities, and develop your rhythmic skills so you can explore many styles of music and interact with other musicians.

Another often overlooked aspect of playing an instrument is your <u>sound</u>. How does each chord that you play sound? Does every note of the chord ring out clearly? Are you picking the strings in order to make the nicest sound? Are you able to switch between chords smoothly so they connect to make a flow in a chord progression? These are questions you should ask yourself. By also spending time developing your own sound you will find you give any music your personal stamp and that people enjoy hearing you because they recognize you, in your music..

Learning to <u>practice efficiently</u> is an art in itself. As an overall concept, break up your practicing with rest periods to give your hands and your mind a rest. The length of practice vs. rest will vary depending on the difficulty of the exercise you are working on. In general a 15-30 minute practice followed by a 10-15 minute rest is a good starting place.

Keep a <u>positive frame of mind</u>. It's easy to get discouraged when starting to play the guitar especially for the first time. Many people set up expectations based on their limited knowledge of music or peer pressure. From all my years as an instructor I have found widely ranging development patterns in students. The ones that end up playing the best are the ones who just keep working, asking questions, solving their problems and finding music to be something they just can't live without.

In this 21st century where the buzz words are "easy" and "instantly" remember that music is an art, not a fast food. It's not about finding the easiest and quickest way to play something by leaving out considerations of sound, technique, understanding of purpose (i.e. music theory) and internal connection with your musical self. We all know this instinctively, but it's important to say it and remember it, as you progress.

In closing I would like to tell you how I see music. Music is a complete universe with many wonderful and fascinating aspects. From the theories of why and how notes go together to the intricate world of rhythm, to the understanding of music from an aural perspective, music gives you a field of study that is vast and rewarding on every level. As you start to understand each musical kernel that makes up the whole, you will be rewarded by this extraordinary world. If you approach your studies of the guitar and music as a life long quest, you will find that it gives you satisfaction, amazement and most importantly joy as you hear and experience this ever unfolding musical cosmos.

Picture 1

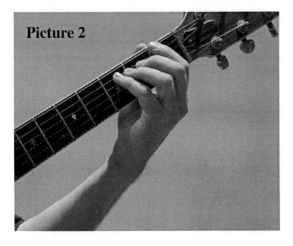

Picture 2

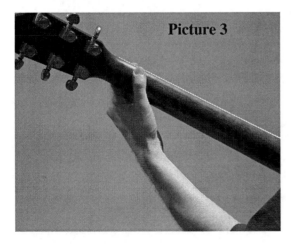

Picture 3

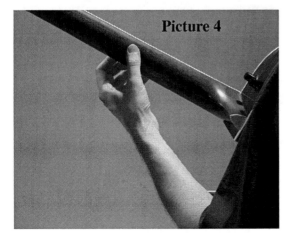

Picture 4

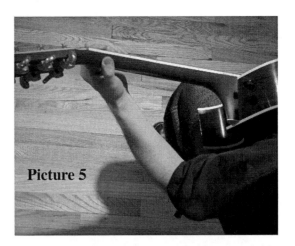

Picture 5

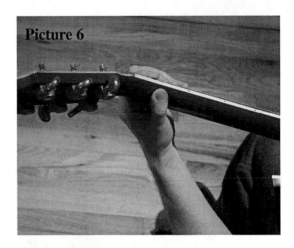

Picture 6

Picture 7

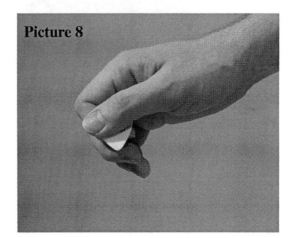

Picture 8

51

Picture 9

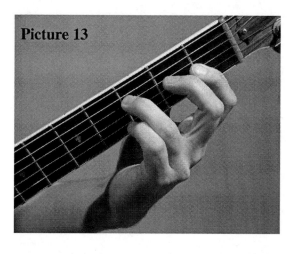

Picture 13

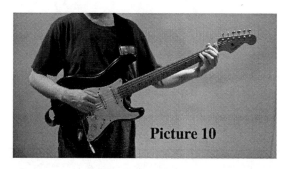

Picture 10

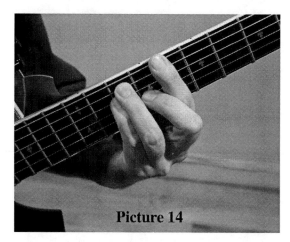

Picture 14

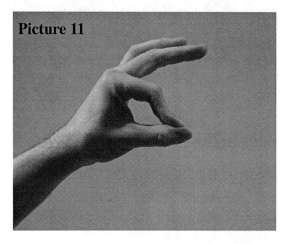

Picture 11

Picture 15

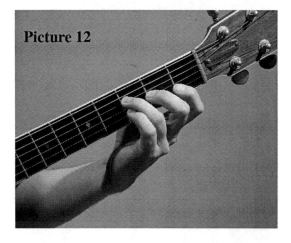

Picture 12

Picture 16

Books Available From
Muse Eek Publishing Company

The Bruce Arnold series of instruction books for guitar are the result of 20 years of teaching. Mr. Arnold, who teaches at New York University and Princeton University has listened to the questions and problems of his students, and written forty books addressing the needs of the beginning to advanced student. Written in a direct, friendly and practical manner, each book is structured in such as way as to enable a student to understand, retain and apply musical information. In short, these books teach.

1st Steps for a Beginning Guitarist
Spiral Bound ISBN 1890944-90-4   Perfect Bound ISBN 1890944-93-9

"1st Steps for a Beginning Guitarist" is a comprehensive method for guitar students who have no prior musical training. Whether you are playing acoustic, electric or twelve-string guitar, this book will give you the information you need, and trouble shoot the various pitfalls that can hinder the self-taught musician. Includes pictures, videos and audio in the form of midifiles and mp3's.

Chord Workbook for Guitar Volume 1 (2nd edition)
Spiral Bound ISBN 0-9648632-1-9   Perfect Bound ISBN 1890944-50-5

A consistent seller, this book addresses the needs of the beginning through intermediate student. The beginning student will learn chords on the guitar, and a section is also included to help learn the basics of music theory. Progressions are provided to help the student apply these chords to common sequences. The more advanced student will find the reharmonization section to be an invaluable resource of harmonic choices. Information is given through musical notation as well as tablature.

Chord Workbook for Guitar Volume 2 (2nd edition)
Spiral Bound ISBN 0-9648632-3-5   Perfect Bound ISBN 1890944-51-3

This book is the Rosetta Stone of pop/jazz chords, and is geared to the intermediate to advanced student. These are the chords that any serious student bent on a musical career must know. Unlike other books which simply give examples of isolated chords, this unique book provides a comprehensive series of progressions and chord combinations which are immediately applicable to both composition and performance.

Music Theory Workbook for Guitar Series

The world's most popular instrument, the guitar, is not taught in our public schools. In addition, it is one of the hardest on which to learn the basics of music. As a result, it is frequently difficult for the serious guitarist to get a firm foundation in theory.

Theory Workbook for Guitar Volume 1
Spiral Bound ISBN 0-9648632-4-3   Perfect Bound ISBN 1890944-52-1

This book provides real hands-on application of intervals and chords. A theory section written in concise and easy to understand language prepares the student for all exercises. Worksheets are given that quiz a student about intervals and chord construction using staff notation and guitar tablature. Answers are supplied in the back of the book enabling a student to work without a teacher.

Theory Workbook for Guitar Volume 2
Spiral Bound ISBN 0-9648632-5-1   Perfect Bound ISBN 1890944-53-X

This book provides real hands-on application for 22 different scale types. A theory section written in concise and easy to understand language prepares the student for all exercises. Worksheets are given that quiz a student about scale construction using staff notation and guitar tablature. Answers are supplied in the back of the book enabling a student to work without a teacher. Audio files are also available on the muse-eek.com website to facilitate practice and improvisation with all the scales presented.

Rhythm Book Series

These books are a breakthrough in music instruction, using the internet as a teaching tool! Audio files of all the exercises are easily downloaded from the internet.

Rhythm Primer
Spiral Bound ISBN 0-890944-03-3   Perfect Bound ISBN 1890944-59-9

This 61 page book concentrates on all basic rhythms using four rhythmic levels. All examples use one pitch, allowing the student to focus completely on time and rhythm. All exercises can be downloaded from the internet to facilitate learning. See http://www.muse-eek.com for details

Rhythms Volume 1
Spiral Bound ISBN 0-9648632-7-8   Perfect Bound ISBN 1890944-55-6

This 120 page book concentrates on eighth note rhythms and is a thesaurus of rhythmic patterns. All examples use one pitch, allowing the student to focus completely on time and rhythm. All exercises can be downloaded from the internet to facilitate learning. See http://www.muse-eek.com for details.

Rhythms Volume 2
Spiral Bound ISBN 0-9648632-8-6   Perfect Bound ISBN 1890944-56-4

This volume concentrates on sixteenth note rhythms, and is a 108 page thesaurus of rhythmic patterns. All examples use one pitch, allowing the student to focus completely on time and rhythm. All exercises can be downloaded from the internet to facilitate learning. See http://www.muse-eek.com for details.

Rhythms Volume 3
Spiral Bound ISBN 0-890944-04-1   Perfect Bound ISBN 1890944-57-2

This volume concentrates on thirty second note rhythms, and is a 102 page thesaurus of rhythmic patterns. All examples use one pitch, allowing the student to focus completely on time and rhythm. All exercises can be downloaded from the internet to facilitate learning. See http://www.muse-eek.com for details.

Odd Meters Volume 1
Spiral Bound ISBN 0-9648632-9-4   Perfect Bound ISBN 1890944-58-0

This book applies both eighth and sixteenth note rhythms to odd meter combinations. All examples use one pitch, allowing the student to focus completely on time and rhythm. Exercises can be downloaded from the internet to facilitate learning. This 100 page book is an essential sight reading tool. See http://www.muse-eek.com for details.

Contemporary Rhythms Volume 1
Spiral Bound ISBN 1-890944-27-0   Perfect Bound ISBN 1890944-84-X

This volume concentrates on eight note rhythms and is a thesaurus of rhythmic patterns. Each exercise uses one pitch which allows the student to focus completely on time and rhythm. Exercises use modern innovations common to twentieth century notation, thereby familiarizing the student with the most sophisticated systems likely to be encountered in the course of a musical career. All exercises can be downloaded from the internet to facilitate learning. See http://www.muse-eek.com for details.

Contemporary Rhythms Volume 2
Spiral Bound ISBN 1-890944-28-9   Perfect Bound ISBN 1890944-85-8

This volume concentrates on sixteenth note rhythms and is a thesaurus of rhythmic patterns. Each exercise uses one pitch which allows the student to focus completely on time and rhythm. Exercise use modern innovations common to twentieth century notation, thereby familiarizing the student with the most sophisticated systems likely to be encountered in the course of a musical career. All exercises can be downloaded from the internet to facilitate learning. See http://www.muse-eek.com for details.

Independence Volume 1
Spiral Bound ISBN 1-890944-00-9   Perfect Bound ISBN 1890944-83-1

This 51 page book is designed for pianists, stick and touchstyle guitarists, percussionists and anyone who wishes to develop the rhythmic independence of their hands. This volume concentrates on quarter, eighth and sixteenth note rhythms and is a thesaurus of rhythmic patterns. The exercises in this book gradually incorporate more and more complex rhythmic patterns making it an excellent tool for both the beginning and the advanced student.

Other Guitar Study Aids

Right Hand Technique for Guitar Volume 1
Spiral Bound ISBN 0-9648632-6-X   Perfect Bound ISBN 1890944-54-8

Here's a breakthrough in music instruction, using the internet as a teaching tool! This book gives a concise method for developing right hand technique on the guitar, one of the most overlooked and under-addressed aspects of learning the instrument. The simplest, most basic movements are used to build fatigue-free technique. Exercises can be downloaded from the internet to facilitate learning. See http://www.muse-eek.com for details.

Single String Studies Volume One
Spiral Bound ISBN 1-890944-01-7   Perfect Bound ISBN 1890944-62-9

This book is an excellent learning tool for both the beginner who has no experience reading music on the guitar, and the advanced student looking to improve their ledger line reading and general knowledge of each string of the guitar. Each exercise concentrates the students attention on one string at a time. This allows a familiarity to form between the written pitch and where it can be found on the guitar along with improving one's "feel" for jumping linearly across the fretboard. Exercises can be downloaded from the internet to facilitate learning. See http://www.muse-eek.com for details.

Single String Studies Volume Two
Spiral Bound ISBN 1-890944-05-X   Perfect Bound ISBN 1890944-64-5

This book is a continuation of Volume One, but using non-diatonic notes. Volume Two helps the intermediate and advanced student improve their ledger line reading and general knowledge of each string of the guitar. Each exercise concentrates the students attention on one string at a time. This allows a familiarity to form between the written pitch and where it can be found on the guitar along with improving one's "feel" for jumping linearly across the fretboard. Exercises can be downloaded from the internet to facilitate learning. See http://www.muse-eek.com for details.

Single String Studies Volume One (Bass Clef)
Spiral Bound ISBN 1-890944-02-5   Perfect Bound ISBN 1890944-63-7

This book is an excellent learning tool for both the beginner who has no experience reading music on the bass guitar, and the advanced student looking to improve their ledger line reading and general knowledge of each string of the bass. Each exercise concentrates a students attention of one string at a time. This allows a familiarity to form between the written pitch and where it can be found on the bass along with improving one's "feel" for jumping linearly across the fretboard. Exercises can be downloaded from the internet to facilitate learning. See http://www.muse-eek.com for details.

Single String Studies Volume Two (Bass Clef)
Spiral Bound ISBN 1-890944-06-8   Perfect Bound ISBN 1890944-65-3

This book is a continuation of Volume One, but using non-diatonic notes. Volume Two helps the intermediate and advanced student improve their ledger line reading and general knowledge of each string of the bass. Each exercise concentrates the students attention on one string at a time. This allows a familiarity to form between the written pitch and where it can be found on the bass along with improving one's "feel" for jumping linearly across the fretboard. Exercises can be downloaded from the internet to facilitate learning. See http://www.muse-eek.com for details.

Guitar Clinic
Spiral Bound ISBN 1-890944-45-9   Perfect Bound ISBN 1890944-86-6

Guitar Clinic" contains techniques and exercises Mr. Arnold uses in the clinics and workshops he teaches around the U.S.. Much of the material in this book is culled from Mr. Arnold's educational series, over thirty books in all. The student wishing to expand on his or her studies will find suggestions within the text as to which of Mr. Arnold's books will best serve their specific needs. Topics covered include: how to read music, sight reading, reading rhythms, music theory, chord and scale construction, modal sequencing, approach notes, reharmonization, bass and chord comping, and hexatonic scales.

Sight Singing and Ear Training Series

The world is full of ear training and sight reading books, so why do we need more?
This sight singing and ear training series uses a different method of teaching relative pitch sight singing and ear training. The success of this method has been remarkable. Along with a new method of ear training these books also use CDs and the internet as a teaching tool! Audio files of all the exercises are easily downloaded from the internet at www.muse-eek.com By combining interactive audio files with a new approach to ear training a student's progress is limited only by their willingness to practice!

A Fanatic's Guide to Ear Training and Sight Singing
Spiral Bound ISBN 1-890944-19-X   Perfect Bound ISBN 1890944-75-0

This book and CD present a method for developing good pitch recognition through sight singing. This method differs from the myriad of other sight singing books in that it develops the ability to identify and name all twelve pitches within a key center. Through this method a student gains the ability to identify sound based on it's relationship to a key and not the relationship of one note to another (i.e. interval training as commonly taught in many texts). All note groupings from one to six notes are presented giving the student a thesaurus of basic note combinations which develops sight singing and note recognition to a level unattainable before this Guide's existence.

Key Note Recognition
Spiral Bound ISBN 1-890944-30-3   Perfect Bound ISBN 1890944-77-7

This book and CD present a method for developing the ability to recognize the function of any note against a key. This method is a must for anyone who wishes to sound one note on an instrument or voice and instantly know what key a song is in. Through this method a student gains the ability to identify a sound based on its relationship to a key and not the relationship of one note to another (i.e. interval training as commonly taught in many texts). Key Center Recognition is a definite requirement before proceeding to two note ear training.

LINES Volume One: Sight Reading and Sight Singing Exercises
Spiral Bound ISBN 1-890944-09-2   Perfect Bound ISBN 1890944-76-9

This book can be used for many applications. It is an excellent source for easy half note melodies that a beginner can use to learn how to read music or for sight singing slightly chromatic lines. An intermediate or advanced student will find exercises for multi-voice reading. These exercises can also be used for multi-voice ear training. The book has the added benefit in that all exercises can be heard by downloading the audio files for each example. See http://www.muse-eek.com for details.

Ear Training ONE NOTE: Beginning Level
Spiral Bound ISBN 1-890944-12-2   Perfect Bound ISBN 1890944-66-1

This is a new method for developing instantaneous recognition of pitches within a key. This contextual-based ear training differs from interval based training by instilling a sense of key relationship; that is, a note is identified by it's characteristic sound within a key, and not by its distance from another note. This method has been used with great success and is now finally available on CD. There are three levels available depending on the student's ability. This beginning level is recommended for students who have little or no music training. A Complete Method book containing the Ear Training One Note Beginning, Intermediate and Advanced levels along with three accompanying CDs is also available for those students wishing to have a complete set of books and CDs under one cover.

Ear Training ONE NOTE: Intermediate Level
Spiral Bound ISBN 1-890944-13-0   Perfect Bound ISBN 1890944-67-X

This is a new method for developing instantaneous recognition of pitches within a key. This contextual-based ear training differs from interval based training by instilling a sense of key relationship; that is, a note is identified by it's characteristic sound within a key, and not by its distance from another note. This method has been used with great success and is now finally available on CD. There are three levels available depending on the student's ability. This intermediate level is recommended for students who have had some music training but still find their skills need more development.   A Complete Method book containing the Ear Training One Note Beginning, Intermediate and Advanced levels along with three accompanying CDs is also available for those students wishing to have a complete set of books and CDs under one cover.

Ear Training ONE NOTE: Advanced Level
Spiral Bound ISBN 1-890944-14-9   Perfect Bound ISBN 1890944-68-8

This is a new method for developing instantaneous recognition of pitches within a key. This contextual-based ear training differs from interval based training by instilling a sense of key relationship; that is, a note is identified by it's characteristic sound within a key, and not by its distance from another note. This method has been used with great success and is now finally available on CD. There are three levels available depending on the student's ability. This advanced level is recommended for advanced music students or those who have worked with the intermediate level and now wish to perfect their skills. A Complete Method book containing the Ear Training One Note Beginning, Intermediate and Advanced levels along with three accompanying CDs is also available for those students wishing to have a complete set of books and CDs under one cover.

Ear Training ONE NOTE: Complete Method
Spiral Bound ISBN 1-890944-47-5   Perfect Bound ISBN 1890944-48-3

This is a new method for developing instantaneous recognition of pitches within a key. This contextual-based ear training differs from interval based training by instilling a sense of key relationship; that is, a note is identified by it's characteristic sound within a key, and not by its distance from another note. This Complete Method book contains the Ear Training One Note Beginning, Intermediate and Advanced levels along with three accompanying CDsand is available for those students who wish to have a complete set of books and CDs under one cover.

Ear Training TWO NOTE: Beginning Level Volume One
Spiral Bound ISBN 1-890944-31-9   Perfect Bound ISBN 1890944-69-6

This Book and Audio CD continues the method of developing relative pitch ear training as set forth in the "Ear Training, One Note" series. There are six volumes in the beginning level series. Through practice, the student eventually gains the ability to recognize the key and the names of any two notes played simultaneously. Volume One concentrates on 5ths. Prerequisite: a strong grasp of the One Note method.

Ear Training TWO NOTE: Beginning Level Volume Two
Spiral Bound ISBN 1-890944-32-7   Perfect Bound ISBN 1890944-70-X

This Book and Audio CD continues the method of developing relative pitch ear training as set forth in the "Ear Training, One Note" series. There are six volumes in the beginning level series. Through practice, the student eventually gains the ability to recognize the key and the names of any two notes played simultaneously. Volume Two concentrates on 3rds. Prerequisite: a strong grasp of the One Note method.

Ear Training TWO NOTE: Beginning Level Volume Three
Spiral Bound ISBN 1-890944-33-5   Perfect Bound ISBN 1890944-71-8

This Book and Audio CD continues the method of developing relative pitch ear training as set forth in the "Ear Training, One Note" series. There are six volumes in the beginning level series. Through practice, the student eventually gains the ability to recognize the key and the names of any two notes played simultaneously. Volume Three concentrates on 6ths. Prerequisite: a strong grasp of the One Note method.

Ear Training TWO NOTE: Beginning Level Volume Four
Spiral Bound ISBN 1-890944-34-3   Perfect Bound ISBN 1890944-72-6

This Book and Audio CD continues the method of developing relative pitch ear training as set forth in the "Ear Training, One Note" series. There are six volumes in the beginning level series. Through practice, the student eventually gains the ability to recognize the key and the names of any two notes played simultaneously. Volume Four concentrates on 4ths. Prerequisite: a strong grasp of the One Note method.

Ear Training TWO NOTE: Beginning Level Volume Five
Spiral Bound ISBN 1-890944-35-1   Perfect Bound ISBN 1890944-73-4

This Book and Audio CD continues the method of developing relative pitch ear training as set forth in the "Ear Training, One Note" series. There are six volumes in the beginning level series. Through practice, the student eventually gains the ability to recognize the key and the names of any two notes played simultaneously. Volume Five concentrates on 2nds. Prerequisite: a strong grasp of the One Note method.

Ear Training TWO NOTE: Beginning Level Volume Six
Spiral Bound ISBN 1-890944-36-X   Perfect Bound ISBN 1890944-74-2

This Book and Audio CD continues the method of developing relative pitch ear training as set forth in the "Ear Training, One Note" series. There are six volumes in the beginning level series. Through practice, the student eventually gains the ability to recognize the key and the names of any two notes played simultaneously. Volume Six concentrates on 7ths. Prerequisite: a strong grasp of the One Note method.

Comping Styles Series

This series is built on the progressions found in Chord Workbook Volume One. Each book covers a specific style of music and presents exercises to help a guitarist, bassist or drummer master that style. Audio CDs are also available so a student can play along with each example and really get "into the groove."

Comping Styles for the Guitar Volume Two FUNK
Spiral Bound ISBN 1-890944-07-6   Perfect Bound ISBN 1890944-60-2

This volume teaches a student how to play guitar or piano in a funk style. 36 Progressions are presented: 12 keys of a Major and Minor Blues plus 12 keys of Rhythm Changes A different groove is presented for each exercise giving the student a wide range of funk rhythms to master.   An Audio CD is also included so a student can play along with each example and really get "into the groove." The audio CD contains "trio" versions of each exercise with Guitar, Bass and Drums.

Comping Styles for the Bass Volume Two FUNK
Spiral Bound ISBN 1-890944-08-4   Perfect Bound ISBN 1890944-61-0

This volume teaches a student how to play bass in a funk style. 36 Progressions are presented: 12 keys of a Major and Minor Blues plus 12 keys of Rhythm Changes A different groove is presented for each exercise giving the student a wide range of funk rhythms to master.   An Audio CD is also included so a student can play along with each example and really get "into the groove." The audio CD contains "trio" versions of each exercise with Guitar, Bass and Drums.

Bass Lines: Learning and Understanding the Jazz-Blues Bass Line
Spiral Bound ISBN 1-890944-94-7   Perfect Bound ISBN 1890944-95-5

This book covers the basics of bass line construction. A theoretical guide to building bass lines is presented along with 36 chord progressions utilizing the twelve keys of a Major and Minor Blues, plus twelve keys of Rhythm Changes. A reharmonization section is also provided which demonstrates how to reharmonize a chord progression on the spot.

Time Series

The Doing Time series presents a method for contacting, developing and relying on your internal time sense: This series is an excellent source for any musician who is serious about developing strong internal sense of time. This is particularly useful in any kind of music where the rhythms and time signatures may be very complex or free, and there is no conductor.

THE BIG METRONOME
Spiral Bound ISBN   1-890944-37-8   Perfect Bound ISBN 1890944-82-3

The Big Metronome is designed to help you develop a better internal sense of time. This is accomplished by requiring you to "feel time" rather than having you rely on the steady click of a metronome. The idea is to slowly wean yourself away from an external device and rely on your internal/natural sense of time. The exercises presented work in conjunction with the three CDs that accompany this book. CD 1 presents the first 13 settings from a traditional metronome 40-66; the second CD contains metronome markings 69-116, and the third CD contains metronome markings 120-208. The first CD gives you a 2 bar count off and a click every measure, the second CD gives you a 2 bar count off and a click every 2 measures, the 3rd CD gives you a 2 bar count off and a click every 4 measures. By presenting all common metronome markings a student can use these 3 CDs as a replacement for a traditional metronome.

Doing Time with the Blues Volume One:
Spiral Bound ISBN 1-890944-17-3   Perfect Bound ISBN 1890944-78-5

The book and CD presents a method for gaining an internal sense of time thereby eliminating dependence on a metronome. The book presents the basic concept for developing good time and also includes exercises that can be practiced with the CD. The CD provides eight 8 minute tracks at different tempos in which the time is delineated every 2 bars, and with an extra hit every 12 bars to outline the blues form. The student may then use the exercises presented in the book to gain control of their execution or improvise to gain control of their ideas using this bare minimum of time delineation.

Doing Time with the Blues Volume Two:
Spiral Bound ISBN 1-890944-18-1   Perfect Bound ISBN 1890944-79-3

This is the 2nd volume of a four volume series which presents a method for developing a musician's internal sense of time, thereby eliminating dependence on a metronome. This 2nd volume presents different exercises which further the development of this time sense. This 2nd volume begins to test even a professional level player's ability. The CD provides eight 8 minute tracks at different tempos in which the time is delineated every 4 bars with an extra hit every 12 bars to outline the blues form.   New exercises are also included that can be practiced with the CD. This series is an excellent source for any musician who is serious about developing an internal sense of time.

Doing Time with 32 bars Volume One:
Spiral Bound ISBN 1-890944-22-X   Perfect Bound ISBN 1890944-80-7

The book and CD presents a method for gaining an internal sense of time thereby eliminating dependence on a metronome. The book presents the basic concept for developing good time and also includes exercises that can be practiced with the CD. The CD provides eight 8 minute tracks at different tempos in which the time is delineated every 2 bars, with an extra hit every 32 to outline the 32 bar form. The student may then use the exercises presented in the book to gain control of their execution or improvise to gain control of their ideas using this bare minimum of time delineation.

Doing Time with 32 bars Volume Two:
Spiral Bound ISBN 1-890944-23-8   Perfect Bound ISBN 1890944-81-5

This is the 2nd volume of a four volume series which presents a method for developing a musician's internal sense of time, thereby eliminating dependence on a metronome..   This 2nd volume presents different exercises which further the development of this time sense. This 2nd volume begins to test even a professional level player's ability. The CD provides eight 8 minute tracks at different tempos in which the time is delineated every 4 bars with an extra hit every 32 bars to outline the 32 bar form.   New exercises are also included that can be practiced with the CD. This series is an excellent source for any musician who is serious about developing an internal sense of time.

Other Workbooks

Music Theory Workbook for All Instruments, Volume 1: Interval and Chord Construction
Spiral Bound ISBN 1890944-92-0   Perfect Bound ISBN 1890944-46-7

This book provides real hands-on application of intervals and chords. A theory section written in concise and easy to understand language prepares the student for all exercises. Worksheets are given that quiz a student about intervals and chord construction using staff notation. Answers are supplied in the back of the book enabling a student to work without a teacher.

E-Books

The Bruce Arnold series of instructional E-books is for the student who wishes to target specific areas of study that are of particular interest. Many of these books are excerpted from other larger texts. The excerpted source is listed for each book. These books are available on-line at www.muse-eek.com as well as at many e-tailers throughout the internet. These books can also be purchased in the traditional book binding format. (See the ISBN number for proper format)

Chord Velocity: Volume One, Learning to switch between chords quickly
E-book ISBN 1-890944-88-2   Traditional Book Binding ISBN 1-890944-97-1

The first hurdle a beginning guitarist encounters is difficulty in switching between chords quickly enough to make a chord progression sound like music. This book provides exercises that help a student gradually increase the speed with which they change chords. Special free audio files are also available on the muse-eek.com website to make practice more productive and fun. With a few weeks, remarkable improvement by can be achieved using this method. This book is excerpted from "1st Steps for a Beginning Guitarist Volume One."

Guitar Technique: Volume One, Learning the basics to fast, clean, accurate and fluid performance skills.
E-book ISBN 1-890944-91-2   Traditional Book Binding ISBN 1-890944-99-8

This book is for both the beginning guitarist or the more experienced guitarist who wishes to improve their technique. All aspects of the physical act of playing the guitar are covered, from how to hold a guitar to the specific way each hand is involved in the playing process. Pictures and videos are provided to help clarify each technique. These pictures and videos are either contained in the book or can be downloaded at www.muse-eek.com This book is excerpted from "1st Steps for a Beginning Guitarist Volume One."

Accompaniment: Volume One, Learning to Play Bass and Chords Simultaneously
E-book ISBN 1-890944-87-4   Traditional Book Binding ISBN 1-890944-96-3

The techniques found within this book are an excellent resource for creating and understanding how to play bass and chords simultaneously in a jazz or blues style. Special attention is paid to understanding how this technique is created, thereby enabling the student to recreate this style with other pieces of music. This book is excerpted from the book "Guitar Clinic."

Beginning Rhythm Studies: Volume One, Learning the basics of reading rhythm and playing in time.
E-book ISBN 1-890944-89-0   Traditional Book Binding 1-890944-98-X

This book covers the basics for anyone wishing to understand or improve their rhythmic abilities. Simple language is used to show the student how to read and play rhythm. Exercises are presented which can accelerate the learning process. Audio examples in the form of midifiles are available on the muse-eek.com website to facilitate learning the correct rhythm in time. This book is excerpted from the book "Rhythm Primer."